4/2/19

FINDING HOPE AND FAITH
IN THE FACE OF DEATH

Seth—
Thanks for your interest in my book!
It's great to be in Cincinnati and to
recall the old neighborhood.
Please share the positive messages
of the book with others

ז"ל

Steve

Finding Hope and Faith in the Face of Death

Insights of a Rabbi and Mourner

Stephen A. Karol

 CASCADE *Books* · Eugene, Oregon

FINDING HOPE AND LIFE IN THE FACE OF DEATH
Insights of a Rabbi and Mourner

Cascade Books
An Imprint of Wipf and Stock Publishers
199 W. 8th Ave., Suite 3
Eugene, OR 97401

www.wipfandstock.com

PAPERBACK ISBN: 978-1-5326-4048-3
HARDCOVER ISBN: 978-1-5326-4049-0
EBOOK ISBN: 978-1-5326-4050-6

Cataloging-in-Publication data:

Names: Karol, Stephen A. (Stephen Allen), author.
Title: Finding hope and life in the face of death : insights of a rabbi and mourner / Stephen A. Karol.
Description: Eugene, OR: Cascade Books, 2018. | Includes bibliographical references.
Identifiers: ISBN: 978-1-5326-4048-3 (paperback). | ISBN: 978-1-5326-4049-0 (hardcover). | ISBN: 978-1-5326-4050-6 (epub).
Subjects: LCSH: Judaism. | Death. | Grief. | Hope. | Consolation.
Classification: BM645 .I5 K36 2018 (print). | BM645 (epub).

Manufactured in the U.S.A.   APRIL 4, 2018

Jillian Levine's poem "Everywhere" is reprinted from *The Living Memories Project: Legacies That Last*, with permission from Little Miami Publishers in Milford, Ohio.

Ann Weems's poem "I See Your Pain" is reprinted from *Searching for Shalom: Resources for Creative Worship*, with permission from Westminster John Knox Press.

Scripture quotations are reproduced from *The Tanakh: The Holy Scriptures* by permission of the University of Nebraska Press, copyright 1985 by the Jewish Publication Society, Philadelphia.

To my wife, Donna, whose love and faith
have taken me to new heights;

To my daughter, Samantha, whose love
and understanding have made me a better person;

To my friend Ray,
whose advice and support have given me hope.

Contents

Preface ix

Introduction xi

1. Accompanying the Dead 1

2. A Harvest of Memories 6

3. God Is Here for You 9

4. Do We Honor Our Dead—Or Worship Them? 14

5. Is Heaven for Real? 19

6. Does the Soul Survive?
   Afterlife, Past Lives, and Living with Purpose 23

7. We are the Ones God Sends 28

8. The Last Lecture 33

9. Are We Something . . . or Nothing? 38

10. To Live a Thousand Years! 42

11. The Freedom to Remember 46

12. What We Can Learn from Death 50

13. Does God Remember? 55

14. Death and Regrets 58

15. The Pain of Losing a Child: In Newtown and among
    Ourselves 63

16. The Mystery of the *Kaddish* 71

Bibliography 75

Preface

Our memories provide sustenance for us. We may wish that things had been different—that our loved ones were still alive, that they had lived longer, and that we had said more to them or done more for them than we did. We may have these wishes, and then realize that we cannot change what has happened.

It is crucial to remember what was, not to imagine what could have been. And then, it is a *mitzvah* to honor our loved ones who have died, to cherish our memories of them and be sustained by those memories, to realize how our lives changed when they died, and to be increasingly aware of how we spend our comparatively brief time on this earth.

We do not have to be recent mourners to understand that our memories, brought back to mind by a communal occasion such as a *Yizkor* (Memorial) service, can bring out the best in us and always sustain us. On this sacred occasion, may our memories be pleasant, providing us with a sense of thankfulness for the past and a real feeling of sustenance for the future.[1]

---

1. Karol, *Letter to Members of Temple Isaiah,* April 2014.

Introduction

Despite my faith in life after death, I am afraid to die. It's the uncertainty that bothers me. I don't like uncertainty in general. How much the more so should it bother me about an existence for which there seems to be no real proof. There is speculation, there are "near-death experiences" that people have that seem to have certain elements in common, and there is unquestioned faith among hundreds of millions of religious people. For some, it is better than life on earth, or it is a reward (or punishment) for our earthly deeds.

I can tell you exactly when my uncertainty started. We were living in Hingham, Massachusetts, and I was serving my second congregation of the three that I served over a period of thirty-seven years. Our daughter, Samantha, had just been born, and her bedroom was across the hall from our bedroom. She would occasionally sing herself to sleep; that's what her mother and I called it. She would hum and sound perfectly happy as she drifted off to sleep with a cassette tape of pleasant music playing in the background. Most of the time, I was amazed at how fortunate I was and we were. All of a sudden one night, I sat up in bed and began to think about what it would be like to not have this kind of happiness, and—even worse—to not be alive! What would it be like? And how would I know? I learned later from a therapist that I was "catastrophizing"—letting my imagination run wild and take me to dark places that were the worst possible scenarios.

This catastrophizing—specifically, about not being alive—still crops up occasionally. But, a combination of faith and therapy have convinced me that there is certainty about this: I have no control over what happens to me after I die, but I *do* have control over what I think and what I feel and what I believe about it. And, I have the ability to share my faith and my hope with others—especially in my role as a rabbi. So, I choose to believe in life after death.

But what if I am wrong? What if I am wrong as a rabbi and a mourner? What if—as some people believe—there is nothing after death? What if there is no World-to-Come? What if there is no reuniting with the souls of the people you loved? What if there is no resurrection of the dead and a chance at a second life? And what if my faith is right? What if the preaching and teaching I have been doing for forty years about enduring hope and endless love is right? What if there *is* something in the World-to-Come that involves being reunited with the souls of the people I loved here on earth? I believe that it is right to have faith. Whenever I delivered a sermon at a memorial service or a eulogy at a funeral, whenever I counseled someone whose loved one had died or taught a class about life after death, I hoped that what I had to say about death would bring my congregants and my students comfort and perspective and confidence. For the most part, having hope and faith has worked for them, and it has worked for me.

I got married for the second time in September of 2016 to a beautiful woman named Donna, who also has a beautiful soul. She believes that we were "meant to be," and that we will be connected after we die because we are *bashert* (predestined to be together). Although I am a little more than seven years older than she is, there is no guarantee that I will die first. But, she is confident that we will be reunited in the World-to-Come, that God is good and will arrange the *shidduch* (match) for us there, and that our souls will experience eternity together. She is incredibly convincing, and I—more of a skeptic about the afterlife than she is—have become a convert to her way of thinking and feeling. It is a happy thought and a happy feeling that forms the foundation of her belief, and I am happy to share it with her.

The following chapters convey important spiritual messages about understanding the value of life, making each day count, cherishing the people we love, and being compassionate toward those who are suffering. Actually, *empathy* is probably a better word than *compassion*. I have found that the best comforters of mourners are those loved ones and friends and clergy who have experienced the same pain and have come through it. That doesn't mean that mourners are totally healed, but it does mean that they understand the journey, and the stops and starts along the way that are natural and difficult, and those that are inspiring and surmountable.

I have been an admirer and disciple of Rabbi Harold Kushner since I read his book *When Bad Things Happen to Good People*. In fact, when I teach about Jewish theology, I refer to myself as a "Kushnerian." I have had the good fortune to hear him speak a few times, and I will never forget his observations one of those times about Job and his friends. As you may know, Job is the man to whom everything terrible happens, and his friends come to visit him and argue with him and accuse him. "While we may not like the substance of their message to him," Rabbi Kushner said at one of those speeches, "at least they were there for him."

That's what this book is about—being there for people at a time of death, and providing some hope and faith for them. Sometimes our words are eloquent. Sometimes our gifts are appreciated. But sometimes we are at our best and we are the most empathetic when we are simply *there*. We don't stay away, and we don't get scared of saying the wrong thing, and we don't worry about how strange it will feel for us to talk about the person who died. I believe that God is there for me in my life, and that my being supportive and helpful to others is what God wants me to do. Occasionally, I can be inspiring to other people. Hopefully, this book will make a positive difference in your life. My father died in 2002 and my mother in 2004. During that time, I haven't heard from them. But I have faith and hope that they will be smiling with pride in the World-to-Come if their son makes a positive difference in your life with this book.

one

Accompanying the Dead

My uncle Harry died last month. I had gone to Kansas City to visit my parents and, hopefully, to help them move from an apartment into an assisted-living facility. Between the time I had made my travel plans and the time I arrived, my uncle had been hospitalized for what the emergency room doctor thought was a heart attack. In doing their morning check-in, the nurses at the assisted-living facility where my uncle had moved in October found him on the floor of his bedroom. Having turned ninety in February, he was used to being in the hospital. Uncle Harry had survived a couple heart attacks, a car accident, eye surgery in January, and numerous other ailments through the years—all of which were recorded precisely in files he kept in his apartment. When I arrived on Saturday evening and stopped by my parents' apartment before going to the hotel where I was going to stay, they told me that the hospital had called them in the afternoon to tell them that my uncle was in critical condition. It appeared that— this time—he would not be coming home.

The next morning, at 4:30, the phone rang in my hotel room. It was my mother, telling me that the hospital had called again and requested that a family member come because it looked like Uncle Harry would not last much longer. My dad was not in great shape and my mom wouldn't leave him alone. So I said, "Of course I'll go." Driving the forty blocks between the hotel and the hospital on a quiet Sunday morning, I didn't need much time to get there. I found my way up to the intensive care unit, introduced myself to the nurses, and was taken into the small room where my uncle was lying in bed, hooked up to machines that told in raw numbers how little of his life was left. For half an hour I basically sat with him, held his hand, talked to him, and watched the monitor tell me that he was about to die. When it happened, I accepted the condolences of the staff and called my parents and my brother to make arrangements, and received a call from the funeral home to set up the funeral on Tuesday.

≈ ≈ ≈

There is no doubt in my mind that what I have just described is all too familiar to those who have had similar experiences when family members or friends have died. Our tradition makes clear that there are *mitzvot* (commandments) pertaining to the time leading up to death, when the death actually occurs, the various periods after death, and the ways we should remember those who have died. In observing these mitzvot, we are doing several things. We are showing respect for the deceased. We are comforting the mourners, or being comforted ourselves as mourners. We are linking to a community of the present and the past. And we are affirming our faith in God and the great value that life has over death.

The Mishnah provides for us a list of some of the most important mitzvot in our tradition. The list is so significant that it appears in our prayer book—in the Shabbat morning service in the *Birkot Hashachar*, the Morning Blessings. That means that, theoretically, we are reminded weekly that doing these mitzvot is an essential ingredient in Jewish life. The list follows the blessing for the study of Torah, with which you may be familiar: "*Baruch Ata Adonai, Eloheinu Melech Haolam, Asher Kidshanu B'mitzvotav V'tzeevanu Laasok B'deevrei Torah.* Blessed is the Eternal our God, Sovereign of the Universe, Who hallows us with the gift of Torah and commands us to immerse ourselves in its words." With that as the frame of reference, this quotation from the Mishnah follows:

"These are the obligations without measure, whose reward, too, is without measure: To honor father and mother, to perform acts of love and kindness, to attend the house of study daily, to welcome the stranger, to visit the sick, to rejoice with bride and groom, to console the bereaved, to pray with sincerity, to make peace where there is strife. And the study of Torah is equal to them all, because it leads to them all."[1]

This message is new for some people, old for others. And I want to tell you why it took on a new level of understanding for me, and how it can be the same for all of us. First, the translation of the opening phrase is not really literal, or at least part of it isn't. The reason for this may be that this phrase alludes to a belief in the World-to-Come, the *Olam Haba*, a belief the early Reform Jews found to be somewhat of a distraction from living the life on earth that has been given to us by God. One literal translation would be, "These are the things that cannot be counted, that a man eats their fruits in this world, and the remainder is stored up for him in the World-to-Come, and these are they." What does it mean to "eat the fruits" of honoring your parents, being loving and kind, attending the house of study daily, welcoming the stranger, visiting the sick, consoling the bereaved, praying with sincerity, and making peace when there is strife? I think it means that the fruits of your labors, the results of your efforts, are there for you to see and enjoy when you perform these mitzvot. And what does it mean when it says "the remainder is stored up for him in the World-to-Come"? It means that even after death you will be rewarded for what you have done during your life.

Two other translation issues arise that are crucial to mention. First, the final line in Hebrew only says, "the study of Torah is equal to them all." It does not actually say that it *leads* to them all. Now, this is not an example of liberal translation for a liberal agenda. In fact, the traditional rabbinic commentaries state that the meaning of the study of Torah being equal to all of them, weighted the same itself as all of them combined, is that *knowing* them is the essential prerequisite to *doing* them. Doing mitzvot without knowing they

1. Frishman, ed., *Mishkan T'filah*, 206.

are mitzvot is better than not doing them. Knowing mitzvot but not doing them is *worse*. And, second, I want to draw your attention to the words translated as "consoling the bereaved." The truth is that the Hebrew words *ulvayat hameit* mean "and accompanying the dead." From the word *ulvayat* comes the word *halvayah*, which means "funeral." So, in Jewish tradition, a funeral is about accompanying the deceased to his or her resting place.

That's what we did two days after my uncle died. With my brother, Rabbi Larry, and I there, we had no need for another rabbi. He came in from Topeka with his wife and son, and my wife and daughter flew in from Boston. My parents were unable to attend on that cold and windy March day because my dad was sick, and my mom wanted to stay with him. But we called them on my cell phone and my daughter and nephew held it up to the mouth of whomever was speaking so that they could hear the funeral. The man from the funeral home was there, of course, and we really expected no one else—despite the obituary in the *Kansas City Star*. After all, my uncle was ninety, had been living alone for many years, and had no friends. Much to our surprise, my dad's and my uncle's first cousin arrived for the graveside ceremony. Then, we met a man my uncle had worked with for many years before retiring twenty-five years ago. Finally, one of my parents' friends from their temple came to support them, and to comfort them as mourners—assuming that they would be attending. With such a small group, almost all of us were pallbearers. And as we walked up the steep hill to the grave, the words *ulvayat hameit* sprang into my brain; we were *truly* accompanying the dead. Many times we all let the cemetery workers accompany our dead to their graves, and we walk behind them and whoever is conducting the service. Occasionally, we have the honor ourselves or give to someone else the honor of being a pallbearer. In this case, we all had the honor of performing the mitzvot, the fruits of which were obvious at the time, the memory of which will last a lifetime, and the reward for which may actually be waiting in the World-to-Come.

Having accompanied many people to their graves—many of whom I didn't know—and having done it for my uncle, I understood why it is included with the other commandments and why it is important in and of itself. Every one of those mitzvot is about community. None of them can be done on a deserted island, and none of them can be done without interacting with other people. The reward of their performance is that you do something positive that affects someone in your community as well as you. They are commandments or unselfish deeds that you can learn about, but it is better that you should do them rather than just talk about them. They are mitzvot that are *hard* to do, that may require some effort. But they are deeds that link you with others, with your heritage, and with God, and they have lasting significance. As we go through life, may we be accompanied by those who love us and care about us, and may we accompany them even when it is hard to do so.

two

A Harvest of Memories

As a native of the Midwest living on the East Coast, I am occasionally asked what it's like there. Sometimes, I simply say, "it's nice" and sometimes I answer the question with another question, like: "What do *you* think it's like?" I've found that Easterners think that it's pretty desolate there, with a lot of farmland and very little "civilization." Where I grew up, it was just the opposite. And, as a result, I know about as much about farming and crops and harvests as any New Yorker from Manhattan or Brooklyn or the Bronx. But, I know enough to be aware of the similarities between an agricultural harvest and the ways our memories work.

It seems to me that a harvest has three functions: to serve as an occasion for celebrating the bounty of Nature, to bring together the best of the crops that have been cultivated, and to sustain the people for whom the crops are so important. To our ancestors who were farmers and to present-day farmers, the importance of the harvest would be unquestioned. And it also without question that we have our own "harvest of memories" for our loved ones.

For our ancestors who lived in the land of Canaan, which later became known as Israel and Judah, the holiday of *Sukkot* (Tabernacles) was the fall harvest. It was then that they would certainly find out whether their hard work in planting the summer crop had paid off or not. A summer drought meant a bleak harvest. But, more often than not, they probably enjoyed a bountiful harvest.

Sukkot, previously a holiday of historical significance commemo-rating the Exodus from Egypt, became an occasion for celebrating. The holiday was seven days long, and the eighth day—*Shemini Atzeret*—was a separate event, a so-called sacred assembly. The harvest, combined with the holiday, provided our ancestors with an occasion for collecting the bounty of Nature, and for thanking God for what they had.

By the same token, this holiday is a special occasion for us. It is one of the four times during the year that we observe Yizkor, following the first on Yom Kippur by less than two weeks. The heightened sensitivity and strong emphasis on remembering on Yom Kippur still prevail on this occasion. While Yizkor is in no way a celebration as a harvest might have been, it is an occasion on which we can give thanks. We can be thankful for the bounty of memories we have of those who are no longer living but who will always be loved. And, it makes remembering easier and more fulfilling when we have an occasion such as Yizkor to make that remembering a regular and special activity. The other important fact about Yizkor is that it's a public occasion, a time when we can share the experience of remembering with others in a communal context.

As in every endeavor of life, our ancestors found that what happened at the time of the harvest was not always perfect. Not all of their crops were successful, and not every plant of a successful crop was the best it could be. But the point of a harvest was to glean the best of each crop and use it for food. In addition, the harvest time—particularly Sukkot—brought out the best in our ancestors morally. They made it a practice to offer the best of their fruits and their cuttings to God. And, they were commanded to leave the four corners of their fields unharvested, to not pick their vineyards bare, and to reserve some of what they had for the poor and the stranger, the widow and the orphan.

Similarly, when we have a harvest of our memories, we tend to recall the best qualities of people and the best experiences we shared with them. We would agree that their lives may not have been perfect, or that their actions may not always have been ex-emplary. But these facts do not deter us from remembering the best about them. The ancient rabbis believed that there was always something positive to say about everyone; that's why they insisted on eulogies at funerals. Neither they nor I would propose to have rose-colored glasses or to create erroneous pictures of people who didn't really exist. Reality is important, but so is the act of remembering. Thinking about loved ones positively brings out the best in us. And just as the harvest benefited our ancestors, so our remembering should benefit us and those close to us.

Finally, the harvest provided sustenance. In a literal sense the products or produce of the harvest kept people alive, giving them physical sustenance. And the harvest must have had some emotional value, too—as a time unlike any other, as an event to be regarded with great anticipation, and as the culmination of one period and the beginning of another. Even in the years when the yield was not the greatest, there still must have been a keen awareness of the cycles and rhythms of Nature, and a sense of comfort because of the ways our people made time sacred.

In the same way, our memories provide sustenance for us. We may wish that things had been different—that loved ones were still alive, that they had lived longer, that we had said more to them or done more for them than we did. We may have these wishes, and then realize that we cannot change what has happened. It is crucial to remember what was, not to imagine what could have been. And then, it is a mitzvah to honor our loved ones who have died, to cherish our memories of them and be sustained by those memories, to understand that our lives changed when they died, and to be increasingly aware of how we spend our comparatively brief time on this earth.

We do not have to be farmers to understand that a harvest is a communal occasion that brings the best to people to enhance their lives and to sustain them. And we do not have to be recent mourners to understand that our memories that are brought back by a communal occasion such as Yizkor can bring out the best in us and always sustain us. May our memories be pleasant, providing us with a sense of thankfulness for the past and a real feeling of sustenance for the future.

three

God Is Here for You

This past Sunday, the temple's Torah study group started to study not one of the books from the Torah but the first one from the Prophets section of the Hebrew Bible—the book of Joshua. Believed by some scholars to have been written around the time when the book of Deuteronomy was written—close to six hundred years after the conquest of the Promised Land—Joshua is a continuation of Deuteronomy from a spiritual and historical standpoint. In the very first chapter, God speaks to Joshua directly with these words: "As I was with Moses, so I will be with you; I will not fail you or forsake you . . . Be strong and resolute; do not be terrified or dismayed, for the Eternal your God is with you wherever you go."[1]

Depending on one's relationship with and beliefs about God—particularly when it comes to death—that could be viewed as a contradiction to mourning or a consolation for it. In dealing with people in mourning situations over the years, I have seen faith strengthened and faith shaken, faith found and faith lost, and faith rediscovered and faith rejected. In his book *Teaching Your Children about God: A Modern Jewish Approach*, Rabbi David Wolpe tells a story that I feel relates to God and mourners of all ages: "One day in class, his teacher asked Barry if God can

1. Josh 1:5b, 9, *JPS Hebrew-English Tanakh*, 457.

do everything. 'No,' said Barry. His teacher thought that perhaps Barry misunderstood the question, so she repeated it. Once again Barry answered, 'No.' 'All right,' said his puzzled teacher. 'Tell me, Barry—just what is it that God cannot do?' Barry answered, 'God can't please everyone.'"[2]

In regard to death, there are various ideas about God's role before, during, and after the death occurs, and they don't please everyone. Sometimes what someone believes before a death affects what they believe during and after the death. Yet, there are also situations when a new insight or a new twist can come about, totally unexpected by the person experiencing it, sometimes brought about by what they say or what they read or what happens to them. I am going to share with you why I agree with Judaism's basic tenet: that God is here . . . now . . . tonight . . . *within* us . . . *among* us . . . *for* us.

From the time of the Bible, Judaism has always regarded God as being one, the Creator of the universe and of humanity, the Source of life and death. God is invisible but not intangible, a Spirit and a Force, far beyond us but also within us. A line in one of our prayers says that God is "as close to us as breathing, yet farther than the farthermost star." In our Yizkor services for the festivals and for Yom Kippur, we have quotations from the Bible, early rabbinic writings, and modern sources. They describe God as "shepherd," "guardian," "keeper," a source of "comfort and hope," the "Source of life," and our "refuge," providing "the embrace of Your wings," and "compassion." Rabbi Wolpe has written: "God designed the world so that every living thing dies. We cannot know for sure why it is that God brought death into the world, but we can speculate . . . Death is certain, and we can only move the margins closer or farther. We are sometimes masters of *when* we die. We can cause or delay death. But *that* we die is God's choice."[3]

Despite this loud and clear message from the rabbis and the sources, there is room for questioning and wondering and philosophizing. Last spring I took our high school students to the

2. Wolpe, *Teaching Your Children*, 220.

3. Ibid., 220, 21.

Holocaust Museum in Washington, DC. No matter what your knowledge of or feelings about the Holocaust are, I recommend that you go there because I think that it will both impress you and touch you deeply. This was my fifth visit, and I spent almost half of the time at the very end, where there is a continuous showing of taped interviews with survivors. One of them is a man named Sam Goldberg, a Polish Jew who lived with a fake identity and also spent some time in a few concentration camps. In one heartrending monologue, he talks about a personal encounter with God about the injustice of this experience, a confrontation about evil very similar to that of Job. He asks God for an answer and gets it, he believes, in the form of another transport of Jews destined to be killed that arrives at his camp.

As a counterpoint to Goldberg's view, Rabbi Larry Kushner offers these thoughts in his book *God Was in This Place & I, I Did not Know:* "The question is not Where was God? But why do human beings do such things . . . God did not die in the Holocaust, only the Deuteronomic idea of a God who, through suspending laws of nature, rewards and punishes people. [That seems now] clearly to be metaphors—never meant to be taken literally . . . All theology after the Holocaust must begin with this acknowledgment."[4]

So, we are encouraged to believe that God can be a source of all that is good for us in death. And, we are aware that we can question God and fairness and evil, and that perhaps we can update our theology. But in doing all of this, I believe that it is important that we not lose sight of the idea that God is here in this temple community, in this building, in this sanctuary, in us as a congregation for this particular service, in you and in me who are here tonight as individual human beings. When I read the prayers at a funeral, included among them are these words: "We need light when gloom darkens our lives. We need fortitude and courage when pain and loss assail us. May we find these in God . . . and in loved ones and companions, who do God's work by binding up the wounds of the stricken."[5] That prayer means so much to me, because I see so

4. Kushner, *God Was in This Place*, 61.
5. Polish, *Rabbi's Manual*, 135.

many examples of people bringing comfort to others. For me, that is proof that God is here.

And our tradition tells us that we are created in the divine image, that there is within each of us a spark of God. Some call it the soul, some the conscience, some our personality. Our being created in the divine image means that we have the capacity to exemplify in our words and in our deeds the best qualities that we ascribe to God. When we do that, we grow closer to God and to our fellow human beings. When we fail to do that, we burn bridges rather than build them. The death of a loved one can deeply affect our connection with God, with our very souls, and with our fellow human beings. When we cherish life, when we honor the memories of our loved ones, when we are here together as a community, then that is proof for me that God is here, too.

I really like Rabbi Wolpe's writing. And so, I want to close with a story he relates:

> There is a wonderful Chasidic story about the child of a rabbi who used to wander in the woods. At first his father let him wander, but over time he became concerned. The woods were dangerous and the father didn't know what lurked there. He decided to discuss the matter with his child. One day, he took him aside and said, "You know, I have noticed that each day you walk into the woods. I wonder, why do you go there?" The boy said to his father, "I go there to find God." "That is a very good thing," the father replied gently. "I am glad that you are searching for God. But, my child, don't you know that God is the same everywhere?" "Yes," the boy answered, "but I'm not."[6]

Sometimes, death turns us into a different person, not the same as we used to be or normally are. Sometimes, it leads us to behave differently, to question, and to despair. Sometimes, we may feel like we are wandering in the woods—seeking God, seeking answers, seeking consolation. There are other people who know what we're going through, whose lives have also been affected by death. Their words and actions can lead us to the knowledge that

6. Wolpe, *Teaching Your Children*, 44.

when we need faith and support, when we need hope and strength, God is here. Look around you. God is here.

four

Do We Honor Our Dead—
or Worship Them?

In his classic book *The Jewish Way in Death and Mourning*, Maurice Lamm wrote these words about the care of the body of someone who has just died:

> A human being is equated with a Torah scroll that was impaired and can no longer be used at religious services. While the ancient scroll no longer serves any useful ritual purpose, it is revered for the exalted function it once filled. Man was created in the image of God and, although the pulse of life is no more, the human form must be respected for having once embodied the spirit of God, and for the character and the personality it housed.[1]

When I read this description recently, I felt that it could easily be interpreted as worship of the dead—something of which I disapprove and of which we should have been taught Judaism disapproves as well. The Torah scroll is unquestionably the most important religious object we have. To equate a deceased human being with it would seem to some Jews to be forbidden. Of course, many statements of similar content have been written by modern and ancient authorities about Jewish mourning customs. And

1. Lamm, *Jewish Way*, 3.

many of those practices place such an emphasis on the deceased that it's possible to question just how much Judaism really emphasizes life over death. So, I want to present the case for worshiping, the case for honoring, and the point of remembering those who have died.

It would be very easy for someone to conclude that we Jews and our tradition seem to worship the dead. According to Orthodox law, death grants a special status to even the meanest of people. Mourners are allowed to ask forgiveness of the deceased and are forbidden from eating, drinking, or smoking in his or her presence, and from making derogatory remarks about the deceased— even though they may be true. Judaism officially discourages open caskets, partly to prevent the possibility of even one negative statement by someone who views the body. And, the eulogy is by its very nature supposed to consist of words of praise. As Lamm says, "although the deceased may have been undistinguished in many ways, and lacking certain moral qualities, there is always a substratum of goodness and decency in all people which can be detected if properly sought."[2]

A skeptic could look at such honor for even the dishonorable and conclude that we Jews, in a way, worship the dead. We name children after them and make donations in their memory. We have tombstones erected, plaques engraved, candles lit, and trees planted to show how revered they are. No matter how happy the holiday may be, we always have a prayer in services specifically to recall them, and we even stand up for it! And, having a service four times a year to pay tribute to our deceased loved ones could also support the skeptic's conclusion. That is third only to Shabbat and Yom Kippur in terms of the number of services for a given purpose.

Yet, the skeptic's case for worship is based, at best, on circumstantial evidence and misinterpretation. First of all, the comparison of the deceased to a Torah scroll is clearly *not* a case of worship, since we honor and respect the Torah instead of worshiping it. In order to truly be an object of worship, someone or something is

2. Ibid., 50.

prayed *to, not about*, as we do in regard to our loved ones. Nor is death worshiped in Judaism. Our religious tradition places such a value on life itself that its main concern in death is the dignity of the deceased and doing only what will bring honor to and retain respect for his or her memory. Another consideration is how we deal with death. As Maurice Lamm has written, "It is only the acceptance of the *reality* of death that enables us to overcome the *trauma* of death."[3]

And, I feel that the reason we do so much to honor the memory of the deceased is that the value we attach to life enables us to find and sustain meaning after someone's death. Naming a child for a relative he or she never knew creates a vital link that spans the generations. A child eventually learns about that person whose name was chosen because of the life he or she lived rather than because of her or his death. The stones, the plaques, the candles, and the trees are tangible tokens of the love and devotion that survive death. And our services—their frequency and their content—reflect the traditional view that there is a point to remembering, as individuals and as a community.

What *is* the point? Remembering is as much an emotional activity as an intellectual exercise. Intellectually, we can remember facts and figures, dates and details, but we do so in a virtually clinical way. When we remember *people*, we generally do so emotionally, calling to mind the feelings we had for them, what they meant to us, or the experiences we shared with them. We may even place them on a pedestal, so to speak, enlarging their positive qualities and forgetting their negative qualities. Or, we may be more realistic about who they were and what they did, recognizing that, by our admitting that they may not have been perfect, we are not desecrating their memory.

We do not worship our dead; we *honor* them. Our remembering is indicative of a love that conquers death, of a devotion that defies separation, of an unselfishness that towers over despair. The human ability to remember, and to express feelings about our memories, and to take actions based on our memories, is very

3. Ibid., 31 (italics original).

much cherished and valued in Judaism. Above all, our remembering loved ones who have died brings an added value to the life they lived and affirms a sense of worth that their death can never erase. In bringing honor to them, we bring honor to ourselves. But the point of it all is for *their* benefit, not for ours.

And sometimes, it can be for the benefit of others. I have been reading a book recently entitled *The Living Memories Project: Legacies That Last,* written by Meryl Ain, Arthur M. Fischman, and Stewart Ain. Having experienced the deaths of their parents over just a few years, they sought some perspective and comfort. Stewart asks: "How could I preserve the positive memories of my mother, when what was fresh in my mind was the incredible suffering she endured?"[4] The book consists of thirty-two tributes by Jews and non-Jews, the famous and not famous, to family members who have died. Among the authors are George Clooney's father, Harry Chapin's daughter, Arthur Kurzweil, one of the sons of Julius and Ethel Rosenberg, the late actor Jack Klugman, and the granddaughter of Babe Ruth. Some of them have established scholarship funds, become motivational speakers, created support groups, and simply gained a wonderful sense of perspective in response to the death of family members. And one of them—Jillian Levine, whose mother died when she was just twelve years old—wrote this poem called "Everywhere," which was read at her wedding:

"*You are everywhere*

You are the daisy in my bouquet

You are the ring on my finger

You are the yellow in the flowers

And the red on my fingernails

You are the sun in our wedding theme

You were my strength in planning this wedding

You are the picture that I carry with me in my bouquet

4. Ain, *Living Memories Project*, 8.

You will be the image dancing in my head when the DJ plays the song "Shout" later tonight

You have become a part of each one of us

You may not be here, but today and always, I feel you everywhere

We invite the souls of all who are deceased—a generation has gone but their light forever brightens the land."[5]

I do not, and did not, worship my parents. My father died twelve years ago—six weeks after I became your rabbi—and my mother died ten years ago on May the sixth. Tonight, I am wearing one of my dad's tie tacks, as I do occasionally, out of respect to his memory. I am carrying my mom's pen in my pocket, a pen that I still use for signing naming certificates and ketubot. In my father's memory Temple Isaiah has a youth scholarship fund that has benefited scores of teenagers in our congregation. In my mother's memory her temple has a Sisterhood leadership training fund that has benefited a number of women who, like her, serve their congregation through their commitment to sisterhood. To worship our dead would be equivalent to placing death above life, and we certainly don't do that. By remembering them, we honor them. By creating opportunities for others, we do what our loved ones would have wanted to do themselves, and we perform mitzvot that have a positive influence and a meaningful impact. May it always be said that we bring blessing to the memory of our loved ones, and that their memory may always be for blessing.

5. Ibid., 169–70.

five

Is Heaven for Real?

O ne of the questions I am asked the most by Christians is whether or not Jews believe in heaven and hell. I tell them that Jewish tradition believes in life after death but does not really use the words *heaven* and *hell* these days to describe places of reward and punishment. Instead, the phrase "the World-to-Come" (*Ha Olam HaBa*) in Hebrew is the one that appears most frequently. One of the questions I am asked most by Jews, too, is whether or not we believe in heaven and hell. When I give them the same answer that I give to Christians, the conversation doesn't necessarily end there. There might be follow-up questions, like, so we don't believe in heaven and hell? Or, so what does it mean to be in the *Olam HaBa*? Or, are my parents, brother, sister, or child aware of me here on earth? Or, will I be reunited in the World-to-Come with the people I love? You shouldn't be surprised that we Jews ask questions and want answers; I'm certainly not. And the way that those questions are asked gives me the feeling that those who are asking have hope that death is not the end, that the uncertainty about life after death will be replaced with certainty, and that they can have the faith that everything will be fine. But, if we only had proof, now *that* would be great!

According to a recent *New York Times* number 1 bestseller, called *Heaven Is for Real: A Little Boy's Astounding Story of His Trip* to *Heaven and Back*, there is proof, and it is good news for those who want to believe. Written by Todd Burpo—pastor of the Crossroads Wesleyan Church in Imperial, Nebraska, wrestling coach for junior high school and high school students, member of the Chase County Public School Board, volunteer firefighter for the town of Imperial, and owner of Overhead Door Specialists—the book was a number-one *New York Times* bestseller in 2010. I found out about it a few weeks ago when I happened to be watching the *Today Show*, and Todd was on with his wife, Sonja, and their twelve-year-old son, Colton.

At the age of four, Colton had to undergo emergency surgery and was clinically dead for three minutes. He survived and gradually began revealing to his parents in a matter-of-fact way that he entered heaven. He was able to look down and see the doctor operating on him, see and hear his father praying by himself in a waiting room, and hear his mother talking to someone on the phone. In addition, Colton's parents suffered through a miscarriage the year before he was born after already having a daughter born several years before him. During one of his instances of recalling his experience in heaven, Colton said that he met his miscarried sister, whom no one had told him about, and his great-grandfather who had died thirty years before Colton was born, and then shared impossible-to-know details about each one of them. Colton saw Jesus riding on a horse and described the Son of God as being very nice and loving children; he talked about having met God Who is really big with a really big chair to sit in, and how the Holy Spirit conveys power from heaven to help us. He remembered people with wings and that his great-grandfather had really big wings and that Jesus wore a white robe with a blue sash. In addition, Colton related to his parents the message from God that there would be a big war on earth and that the people who believed in him and Jesus would be okay.

The fact that I found this book in a local bookstore in the Christian section under a sign marked Christian Reading for Easter was not a surprise to me. This book clearly affirms Christian beliefs about the afterlife, God, Jesus, and judgment day. But what does Judaism believe? And how can I answer that question, which is worth an entire course or at least an hour-long lesson in my tenth-grade and adult confirmation classes, in just a few minutes? I can answer it briefly. The Bible mentions Sheol, a place located beneath the earth at the base of high mountains. It was thought to be dark and silent; the dead could not reach out to God from there, but no punishment was connected with the place. This belief existed for at least seven centuries, and when the Bible was canonized in the first century CE, rabbinic writings began to speak about the resurrection of the body and the soul. The Pharisees believed in resurrection and the Sadducees did not, and it was the pharasaic doctrine that survived and thrived. The term *Sheol* was a vestige of the past, and new terminology came into being. The *Olam HaBa* was where and when the righteous would be rewarded and the wicked would be punished, although there was an extremely broad definition of who could be called righteous. *Gan Eden*, or the Garden of Eden, also identified as Paradise, was set against *Gehinnom*, named after the valley in Jerusalem where the Canaanites sacrificed their firstborn children within the earshot of our shocked ancestors. The term *techiyat hamaytim* (the resurrection of the dead) grew as a belief that the souls of the dead would be revived when the Messiah came. And what did those souls do until the arrival of the Messiah? A book called the Wisdom of Solomon says, "But the souls of the righteous are in the hand of God, and no torment will ever touch them. In the eyes of the foolish, they seem to have died, and their departure was thought to be an affliction, and their going from us to be their destruction, but they are at peace."[1]

And, that is what *we* would like to believe—that our family members and friends who have died are at peace. Growing up in a Reform congregation, I was not attuned to the traditional Jewish belief about the resurrection of the dead at some future time. In our version of the *G'vurot* prayer—as it is now in our prayer book *Mishkan T'filah*—we praise God Who gives life to everything, not Who resurrects the dead. I learned about the immortality of the soul, reflected in the ability of loved ones and friends to

1. Quoted in Sonsino and Syme, *What Happens after I Die?*, 40.

remember the person who died, in our realizing that he or she had bequeathed a moral legacy to us, and in our believing that he or she was with us in spirit when we celebrated happy occasions in our lives. If you think that such a Reform belief was beyond the normative Jewish beliefs, consider that the great medieval philosopher Moses Maimonides wrote, "In the World to Come, there is nothing corporeal and no material substance; there are only souls of the righteous without bodies—like the ministering angels. The righteous attain to a knowledge and realization of truth concerning God to which they had not attained while they were in the murky and lowly body."[2]

I as a Jew would like to believe that the *Olam HaBa* is for real—that souls are attaining knowledge, being close to God, feeling no pain, aware of what is happening on earth, and communicating somehow with those who are living. Wouldn't you like to believe the same? I am fascinated by the boy Colton's story, and I find it interesting and somewhat refreshing that the book wasn't written until seven years after his experience with death and heaven. I cannot logically explain how he knew about his sister who died, or how he could describe his great-grandfather in such vivid detail to his parents, never having heard about his sister, and never having seen a picture of his great-grandfather. I can't figure it out any better than I can when people say that they had past lives. But I do know this: having hope about life after death doesn't have to come from a just-right-for-Easter book in the Christian section of Barnes & Noble. That hope can come from the prayers of Yizkor, from the Shabbat prayers that we read when you are at your temple to observe a yahrzeit, and from the prayers of the funeral and burial services of Judaism. They speak of good and love, hope and faith, compassion and peace, life and afterlife. Heaven is *very* real for Colton Burpo, his family, and the hundreds of thousands of people who have read the book. The *Olam HaBa* can be real for you, too, if you choose to believe.

2. Ibid., 41.

six

Does the Soul Survive?

Rabbi, I had an experience that I want to tell you about. One night I had a very vivid dream in which my brother, who died several years before, appeared to me and said that something important was going to happen. I was so startled by the intensity and vividness of the dream and the message that I awoke and sat on the edge of my bed. Soon the phone rang. It was my family thousands of miles away. They told me that my father had just died of a sudden heart attack. Neither I nor they had any indication that he had even been sick.[1]

Your father is here and your son, who is a small child. Your father says you will know him because his name is Avrom, and your daughter is named after him. Also his death was due to his heart. Your son's heart was also important, for it was backward, like a chicken's. He made a great sacrifice for you out of his love. His soul is very advanced . . . His death satisfied his parents' debts. Also he wanted to show you that medicine could only go so far, that its scope is very limited.[2]

1. Spitz, *Does the Soul Survive?*, 6.
2. Ibid., 59–60.

A few years ago I was in a very serious car accident. My
car was totaled, and I was lying unconscious on the side
of the road. It was as if I was no longer in my body. I
looked down and could see myself bleeding. Paramedics gathered around me, and I was drawn toward a light
along with a feeling of great calm. At a certain point I
was given a choice to return to my body and did so. All
of a sudden I became aware of my bodily pain, but my
life was changed. Somehow in that moment I both lost
the fear of death and began to appreciate that each day
is a gift.[3]

These three anecdotes are presented in a book called *Does
the Soul Survive? A Jewish Journey to Belief in Afterlife, Past
Lives & Living with Purpose*. Written by a Conservative rabbi,
Elie Kaplan Spitz, and published by Jewish Lights, it is not only
intriguing but also scholarly in its consideration of whether death
is actually final or not. With a foreword by Brian Weiss, author
of *Many Lives, Many Masters*, and with a chapter devoted to psy-
chic medium James Van Praagh, it would be easy to regard this
book as the wishful thinking of a California rabbi. That would be
a colossal mistake. Rabbi Spitz discusses the soul, survival of the
soul, afterlife, resurrection, and how we should live our lives. And
while I don't agree with everything he says, I believe firmly that the
soul survives death, that there is an afterlife, that there are times
when we can sense the presence of deceased family members and
friends, and that the dead survive in more than our memories.

What is the soul? Rabbi Spitz refers to the three terms for
"soul" in Hebrew—*nefesh, ruach*, and *neshamah*—in explaining
its meaning, and these are the exact terms about which I have
spoken and taught over the years. *Nefesh*, he says, "represents the
realm of action and physical pleasure, [and] supports and connects with *ruach*, the realm of feelings, which enables personality
and the expression of love."[4] *Neshamah* consists of "uniquely human capacities . . . analytic thought, the quest for meaning, and

3. Ibid., 10.
4. Ibid., 25.

transcendence."[5] He believes, as I do, that there are different levels to our souls. I believe that we are born with our souls, which are implanted in our bodies by God at birth. Our souls are truly who we are—our personality, our uniqueness, the voice of conscience, the spark of the Divine within us—and they cannot be seen if you stand in front of an x-ray machine. The Babylonian Talmud says, "As God fills the whole world, so also the soul fills the whole body. As God sees, but cannot be seen, so also the soul sees but cannot be seen. As God nourishes the whole world, so also the soul nourishes the whole body."[6] You and I and the people we mourn were all blessed with a soul.

What does survival of the soul mean? The Torah says that when Abraham died, he was "gathered to his kin."[7] The exact same phrase is used for his sons Ishmael and Isaac, and for Jacob, Aaron, and Moses. Since the Torah tells later of their burials, and of their burials in different places, the phrase doesn't always mean that they were all placed in the same tomb. Our ancestors then believed that, when they died, they were reunited with their family members who had died before them. Unlike some other peoples, the Israelites did not worship or glorify death, did not have a caste system when it came to burial, and did not see death as better than life on earth. They promulgated many laws about contact with human corpses and about eating animals that had been torn apart. And, some two thousand years ago, the rabbis in Palestine began to speak about the reward for a righteous life in this world in the World-to-Come. In other words, death was not the end. We affirm this belief at a funeral and at a Yizkor service. We have the image of a compassionate God, who resides above us, granting "perfect peace in Your embrace . . . so that his/her/their soul may be bound up in the bond of life eternal. May he/she/they find a home with You, and may he/she/they rest in peace. Together we say: *Amen*"[8]

5. Ibid., 25.

6. Babylonian Talmud, *Berakhot* 10a.

7. Gen 25:7, *JPS Hebrew-English Tanakh*, 47.

8. Goor, *For Sacred Moments*, 35, in the section called "Mourning."

There is a third belief in Judaism where some of us part ways with the tradition, and that is resurrection. The Mishnah says, "All of Israel has a place in the world to come, and the following have no portion in the world to come: one who says, 'there is no resurrection of the dead.'"[9] Our most recent prayer book for the Reform movement, *Mishkan T'filah*, has more than one form of the *G'vurot* prayer, whose traditional version mentions resurrection. We now have the option of saying, *mechayei meitim* (reviving the dead) rather than *mechayei hakol* (giving life to all). as in previous prayer books.[10] This is not the first time in our history that there has been disagreement about whether or not we will be resurrected. The Sadducees and the Pharisees differed over this issue two thousand years ago. Reform Judaism rejected the literal, miraculous characterization of resurrection prominent in Orthodox theology. Today some people take the traditional term and interpret it to mean that God makes the dead live again through our own memories and our own deeds. We give life to those who have died when we name children after them, when we say Kaddish on their yahrzeit, and when we do tzedakah or some other mitzvah in their honor. Rabbi Spitz himself writes, "I relate to resurrection metaphorically as a description of a future time in which the world will be renewed and reordered. In that light, the end of days will not mark the resurrection of individuals but global wholeness.[11] He also devotes two chapters to reincarnation. For us, the chance to live more than once may be desirable for ourselves or for our deceased loved ones on some emotional level. But I believe we cannot count on it, nor can we base our lives on the anticipation of getting a second chance.

What then can we believe about our lives and the lives of our loved ones who have died? We can believe that our soul is there, inside of us, our inner connection to God, and it motivates our outer connection to others throughout our lives. No matter what the person you mourn looked like, it is his or her soul with which

9. Mishnah, *Sanhedrin* 11a.
10. Frishman, ed., *Mishkan T'filah*, 246.
11. Spitz, *Does the Soul Survive?*, 54.

you can feel a link. We can believe that our souls and their souls endure beyond death, that they are reunited with God. Whether or not we believe in telepathic episodes like the one I quoted earlier, we can believe that we continue to be influenced by the love we felt for those who have died, by their words or their deeds or their personalities. We can believe that life is a gift, a blessing from God, that we should appreciate the lives of those who have died, and that we should be thankful for the life we have and live it honorably.

I want to conclude with an image from the Kabbalah, the mystical tradition of Judaism, which Rabbi Spitz cites near the end of his book. It is an image in which I believe strongly, and I hope that you will think about it as you consider what you do with your life and how you remember the lives of the deceased: "the kabbalah used the image of fire to convey that all aspects of our life—the physical, emotional, intellectual, and intuitive—are united in soul just as the colored bands [of fire] are united in the flame. Our task is to nurture the flame so that it burns brighter, enabling a greater unity within us, which in turn instills a feeling of being more fully alive and prompts service on behalf of the source of life."[12]

Does the soul survive? I believe it does. Is there an afterlife? I believe there is. Do we live more than once? I don't know. Can and should we live with purpose? *Most definitely!* And, may we use our souls to nurture the flame, as God and our loved ones would want us to do.

12. Ibid., 160.

seven

We Are the Ones God Sends

We gather together at our Yizkor (memorial) services for a common purpose—to honor the memories of loved ones through the ritual of communal remembering. When we do, we fit into three categories of mourners: those who have experienced a death in the last few months, those who have experienced a death in the last year, and those who have experienced a death or more than one death over a period of years. If we were to be constituted as a support group rather than a group of people praying, we would take the opportunity to sit and tell our stories, to talk about the people for whom we mourn, to reflect on the feelings we have had as a result of their deaths, and to share the insights that we have gained in the process. All of that would be the key to making each one of us believe that "I am not alone," "my experience is not unique," "there are other people who know what I am talking about," and "I am among those who think that my reactions to death are normal."

When we pray in a synagogue, our verbalizing is through the language of our tradition and through the structure of our service. It is based on the assumption that there is a God in Whom we believe and Who, in turn, listens to us when we pray and answers those prayers in one way or another. Every Yizkor service is an opportunity for you to affirm that you are connected, that you are not alone, that your experience is not unique, that others know what you're talking about when you mention a loved one who has died, and that those others think that you are as normal as they are. You also have the chance to connect with others after the service, if you choose to stay. I believe, with all my mind and heart and soul, that we can be of help to one another in dealing with death in general and with the death of loved ones in particular. My beliefs are summarized in this reading, written by Ann Weems, called "I See Your Pain":

> I see your pain
> And want to banish it
> With the wave of a star,
> But have no star.
> I see your tears
> And want to dry them
> With the hem of an angel's gown,
> But have no angel.
> I see your heart fallen to the ground
> And want to return it
> Wrapped in cloths woven of rainbow,
> But have no rainbow.
> God is the One
> Who has the stars, and angels, and rainbows,
> And I am the one
> God sends to sit beside you
> Until the stars come out
> And the angels dry your tears
> And your heart is back in place,
> Rainbow blessed.[1]

The pain that you experience because of a death can be emotional or physical, solitary or shared, sudden or prolonged. It can leave its mark in a way that can seemingly never be healed, or it can be lessened by a belief that we can be healed by life itself. The

1. Weems, *Searching for Shalom*, 23.

pain that you experience because of a death is forever etched into your memories and your souls because of the love you felt for the person who has died. And every time you think of that person, and feel a pang of remorse or a tinge of regret or a moment of remembering, you may feel that you're giving in to the pain and that it will never leave you. In those times, you may feel like you want to banish the pain with the wave of a star.

We are the ones God sends to sit beside you until the stars come out again. All of us who have experienced the pain of death know that such pain cannot be *totally* banished—by ourselves, by our friends, by a star, not even by God. It is not the wave of a star, the sense of something magic, or the reliance on something miraculous that helps us deal with pain. It is the presence of others who are there when we need them, who help us when we haven't even asked, and who are silent when we just want to vent. And I don't believe that they are sent by God to take the place of God. I believe that, when each of them acts to sit beside another person until the stars come out, they are acting in a Godly way.

The tears that you cry because of a death may be private or public, periodic or persistent, many or few. Crying can be regarded as a sign of weakness and the inability to cope, or as a sign of healthy emotions and the ability to face reality. The tears that you cry because of a death are because of the love you felt and still feel for the person who died, a love that our funeral ceremony praises as being stronger and more powerful than death. And any time you cry when you think of that person, and you recall what you said on a certain occasion or didn't say, what you did or didn't do, you may feel that the crying is permanent, and that the tears will never end. In those times, you may want to dry those tears with the hem of an angel's gown.

We are the ones God sends to sit beside you until the angels dry your tears. Actually, I believe that it is *we* who are the angels. All of us who have experienced the pain of a death know that tears are inevitable, and most of us realize that they are natural. They are not necessarily a sign of weakness and the inability to cope. In fact, they can serve a cleansing function for our bodies and our souls. It is not the angel of a biblical story or a movie who will come to console you. It is a true angel, a true *malach*, a messenger in human form. It is a relative or a friend, a child or an adult, a clergyperson or a health professional, who will literally sit beside you or across from you, who will reach out to you on the phone or with a note, or who will engage you in a lengthy conversation rather than just asking how you are and not listening to the answer. I don't believe that God sends winged angels from on high to dry our tears. I believe that, when each of us acts to dry someone else's tears, then it is *we* who are angels, behaving as God would want us to behave.

The tear in your heart that you experience because of a death can be immediate or delayed, constant or sporadic, expected or surprising. It is recognized in our ritual with the tearing of a *shiva* ribbon, which we explain as meaning that material things are insignificant to us in comparison to death, but also as meaning that the physical damage done to that small piece of cloth is like the emotional damage done to us. To me, the idea that your heart may fall to the ground or feel torn because of the death of someone you loved indicates a sense of giving up hope and giving in to the grief. Some damage, you may think, can never be repaired. Some things, you may believe, may fall and never be picked up.

We are the ones God sends to sit beside you until your heart is back in place. It may not be in the same place as before, and it may not be in the same shape as before. It is not put back in place by a miracle or an angel because you merely sit there waiting for it to happen, or because someone else is merely sitting next to you waiting for it to happen. It is put back in place because God has put within each of us the power to draw on faith and courage, determination and perseverance, resilience and optimism. It is put back in place when we take advantage of the sense of partnership that is available to us—involving ourselves, others, and God—to wrap that naked and vulnerable heart in the clothing of hope, to pick up the heart that has seen only the color of black, and to remember that the world in which we live is a rainbow.

God is the One who has stars and angels and rainbows. But we are the ones God sends to sit beside you until the stars come out, and the angels dry your tears, and your heart is back in place. When that happens, we are, indeed, "rainbow blessed." We, who feel cursed by death and because of death, can feel blessed because of what God has implanted within us, because of what others can bring us, and because of what we can do. Look for the ones God has sent to sit beside you, be among the ones God has sent to sit beside others, and you will discover the blessing of seeing the world in its true colors.

eight

The Last Lecture

Have you ever seen a dying man doing push-ups? Have you ever seen a dying man doing push-ups in which he does them not with both arms at once, but alternating between his right and left arms? Have you ever seen a dying man doing push-ups with both his arms and clapping his hands after each push-up? Have you ever seen a dying man do all of this in a college auditorium in front of hundreds of people? Have you ever seen a dying man being interviewed about his impending death and his last lecture by Diane Sawyer on ABC-TV? If your answer to any of these questions is yes, then you are familiar with the story of Randy Pausch, the professor at Carnegie Mellon University in Pittsburgh who died from pancreatic cancer at the age of forty-seven in July of 2008. A friend of mine had told me about him several months earlier and then gave me his book *The Last Lecture* on the day Pausch died. What he said in the lecture and wrote in the book resonated with me as a man, a Jew, and a mourner. His multifaceted message is not just good television or good reading, but it is almost word for word what our famous ethical treatise *Pirke Avot* has to say. And, it is a message that can be about those we mourn and about us.

Randy Pausch was a computer science professor who specialized in virtual reality software programs and trained his students to collaborate and create amazing projects. Married at the age of thirty-nine, he and his wife, Jai, had three children—Dylan, Logan, and Chloe. It was for them that he delivered the lecture, titling it "Really Achieving Your Childhood Dreams." As he tried to convince his wife of the importance of the lecture—scheduled for one month after he received a fatal diagnosis—he told her, "This lecture will be the last time many people I care about will see me in the flesh . . . I have a chance here to really think about what matters most to me, to cement how people will remember me, and to do whatever good I can on the way out."[1] He told his audience that he embraced every moment he had, that engineering (especially of the human body) wasn't about perfect solutions but about doing the best you can with limited resources. He felt that it was great to be alive regardless of the results of his tests, and that he was going to make every day count. As an expert on time management as well, he knew about the importance of having a plan but also having a plan B if you had to change. And he was interested in knowledge and actions. "Smart isn't enough," he said. "The kind of people I want on my research team are those who will help everyone else feel happy to be here."[2] He wanted to teach his students and his children, "Go out and do for others what somebody did for you."[3] And he also taught that "everyone has to contribute to the common good. To not do so can be described in one word: selfish . . . When we're connected to others, we become better people."[4]

For Jews an excellent resource of ethics is the *Pirke Avot* (Chapters of the Fathers), which consists of six chapters from the Mishnah with sayings from a number of rabbis over a period of five hundred years. They have been studied for centuries—including in the synagogues at which I have served—and have been quoted in sermons and classes and books for the same amount of time. On two topics I see a similarity between what Pausch said and what is in *Pirke Avot*. One pertains to time, and the other is about wisdom and deeds. The rabbis seemed to agree on the value of time

1. Pausch, *Last Lecture*, 7
2. Ibid., 118
3. Ibid., 158
4. Ibid., 176

and the urgency of it. Hillel said, "Don't say, 'When I have leisure, I will study'—perhaps you never will have that leisure."[5] Eliezer said, "Repent one day before your death."[6] The implications of these sayings, of course, is that we need to think about our words and actions every day, because we don't know when we're going to die. Rabbi Tarfon said, "The day is short; there is much work [to be done]; [yet,] the laborers are lazy, [even though] the wages are great and the Householder is insistent."[7] I believe that these sayings mean that there is a lot that can be done in the short time we have on earth. We may just not want to do it, but the rewards are great, and God wants us to do what we can while we can. And one of my favorites is this one from Rabbi Tarfon again: "It is not up to you to finish the work, yet you are not free to avoid it."[8] We may feel that so much needs to be done to improve our world, but we don't have to do everything on our own. And we shouldn't be so overwhelmed that we do nothing.

And just as wisdom and deeds were important to Pausch, so they were to the Rabbis. For example, Chanina ben Dosa used to say, "One whose deeds exceed one's wisdom, one's wisdom will last. One whose wisdom exceeds one's deeds, one's wisdom will not last."[9] Ben Zoma said, "Who is wise? The one who learns from everyone . . . Who is mighty? One who controls one's [natural] urges . . . Who is rich? One who is happy with what one has . . . Who is honored? One who honors others."[10] In other words, smart isn't enough: we should do for others, and we should connect with others in a positive way.

As mourners, we can reflect on Pausch's message and the words of the *Pirke Avot* in two ways. First, we can think about them in regard to the loved ones we mourn. Whether they knew or didn't know when they would die, did your loved one or friend

5. Kravitz and Olitzky, eds., *Pirke Avot*, 20

6. Ibid., 26.

7. Ibid., 29.

8. Ibid., 30.

9. Ibid., 42.

10. Ibid., 56.

value their time on earth, appreciate the gift of life, and make every day count? Did he or she postpone doing something, thinking that there will always be time to do it? Did she or he speak before acting or act before speaking? Was there a lot accomplished in a short time, and were the rewards great? Did he or she do what they could when they could? Was the person you loved known for wisdom more than deeds, deeds more than wisdom, or both in equal parts? Did he learn from others and control his temper? Was she happy with her life, and did she honor other people? Did the people we remember separate themselves from the community, or did they leave us a legacy?

As individuals, as family members, and as mourners, we need to think of our legacy as well. On our own or because of the influence and example of the people we have loved, we should value life and cherish the time we have, and we should take on responsibilities and not try to fulfill them alone. Although we may feel limited in our resources, we have the ability to give meaning to what we do. Sometimes we live our lives very conscious of what our parents, siblings, spouses, or friends did. As a result, we are determined either to avoid their mistakes or to replicate their successes. Sometimes, we would like to channel their talents and behave like they would in a given situation, and sometimes we would like to be independently creative and be our own person. Like Randy Pausch, we may want those we love or those we care about to be motivated by what we have said or done. And sometimes we need a little bit of perspective. Pausch writes:

> When I was studying for my Ph.D., I took something called "the theory qualifier," which I can now definitely say was the second worst thing in my life after chemotherapy. When I complained to my mother about how hard and awful the test was, she leaned over, patted me on the arm and said, "We know just how you feel, honey. And remember, when your father was your age, he was fighting the Germans." After I got my Ph.D., my mother

took great relish in introducing me by saying: "This is my son. He's a doctor, but not the kind who helps people."[11]

The truth is that Mrs. Pausch's boy became the kind of person who helps people—millions of them, actually. He has helped them just as *Pirke Avot* has helped Jews over the centuries to understand. As Pausch said, "we cannot change the cards we are dealt, just how we play the hand";[12] and, "no matter how bad things are you can always make them worse. At the same time, it is often within your power to make them better."[13]

Judaism believes that God has given us the power to give meaning to our lives and to find meaning in the deaths of those we loved. That is a sense of perspective that should be not only our legacy but also our way of living.

11. Pausch, *Last Lecture*, 24.
12. Ibid., 17.
13. Ibid., 88.

nine

Are We Something . . . or Nothing?

In the vast traditional literature of Judaism, there are many say-ings, proverbs, legends, and parables. Among them are the in-credible writings and oral teachings of the Hasidic rabbis. Simcha Bunim Bonhart (1765–1827) was one of them, and he once said: "Everyone must have two pockets, with a note in each pocket, so that he or she can reach into the one or the other, depending on the need. When feeling lowly and depressed, discouraged or dis-consolate, one should reach into the right pocket, and, there, find the words: 'For my sake was the world created.' But, when feeling high and mighty, one should reach into the left pocket, and find the words: 'I am but dust and ashes.'"[1]

For me this is an example of providing two extremes in order to convey a message. We can feel haughty and full of ourselves, and we can feel insignificant and worthless, and those feelings can be constant or temporary, obvious or subtle. I believe that this gem emphasizes that we should have a sense of perspective and balance in our minds and our emotions. And it is particularly relevant in answering the question, are we something . . . or nothing? Where does that question come from? And, how can we answer it?

The question arises from one of the readings in the memorial service from *The Gates of Prayer*:

1. Buber, *Tales of the Hasidim*, 2:249–50.

"Lord, what are we, that You have regard for us? What are we, that You are mindful of us? We are like a breath; our days are as a passing shadow; we come and go like grass which in the morning shoots up, renewed, and in the evening fades and withers. You cause us to revert to dust, saying: 'Return, O mortal creatures!'"[2]

The reading is a combination of verses from Pss 144 and 90. In context, Ps 144 is a praise of God and petition for God's protection. Ps 90, credited to Moses, compares humanity's brief time on earth to God's permanence. It's possible to read these verses as a put-down of humanity and as a depressing and cynical recognition that life is so short as to be without value. But that is not how they are intended. Ps 144 concludes on a positive note, with the words "Happy the people whose God is the Lord."[3] And, Ps 90 has a positive message later on too: "Teach us to count our days rightly, that we may obtain a wise heart."[4] So, these psalms stress faith in God and making our time on earth count.

I want to consider the Something or Nothing question in reverse order because, especially when a death occurs and we are reminded of our limitations, negative feelings can result. It can be difficult and even disturbing to think about death, to think about the nothingness it represents, and the void it creates in the minds and hearts of those who are mourners. Death can make some people feel so low that they begin to think philosophically in ways they never have before. They may wonder about the value and fairness of life, and about the righteousness of a God Who they believe permits death to happen to their loved ones. Confronted with the mortality of a family member or friend, they see their own mortality clearly and would prefer not to have been reminded of it. They may even lose faith in God, in themselves, and in life because of the circumstances or timing of a death. Or, they may believe that someone else's death is God's way of punishing them and telling them that they weren't good enough to deserve a longer life for their loved one. The death of a good person, the death of

2. Stern, ed., *Gates of Prayer*, 548.
3. Ps 144:15, *JPS Hebrew-English Tanakh*, 1592.
4. Ps 90:12, *JPS Hebrew-English Tanakh*, 1527.

someone "before their time," the death of a child before a parent, the death that occurs suddenly or under violent circumstances or after a painful disease—all are deaths that can potentially lead a person to conclude that we are definitely nothing. In each instance, there is a desire to change what cannot possibly be changed. And there is a failure to recognize that death is inevitable, and that we have no choice but to accept that fact of life.

On the other hand, death can remind us that we are something. We live, we breathe, we think, we feel, we love. We share, we care, we help, we hope, we dream. We human beings, unlike the animals, have the ability to find meaning in life, and we have the ability to recover from someone's death. We have the power of memory that assures that our loved ones live on in our hearts and minds. It is exemplified in what the funeral service says is "a love stronger than death."[5] The pain we feel after a death is indicative of how much we value life, and our religious tradition has always stressed that value. Judaism does not glorify death over life or create detailed speculation about life after death—although there are some exceptions. It has always emphasized that we should make our days count, not take them for granted, and realize that they are limited.

When I deliver a eulogy at a funeral, I try my best to praise the deceased. Rather than delivering what could amount only to an obituary full of facts and figures, I seek to remind the mourners of what made their loved one's life precious, special, and meaningful. Thus, in the face of death, I talk about life and hope. One person's life has ended, but the lives of others must go on. I believe that it is because we feel that life adds up to something that we are able to go on. And I believe that while God has created a universe in which all of God's creations live and die, it is not God Who causes death directly in order to teach us a lesson or force us to find meaning. We alone can find meaning in death, and God has given us the ability to do that. We may change our priorities or lifestyle. We may try to incorporate the qualities of the deceased into how we act, or we may attempt to complete the work they began.

5. Goor, *For Sacred Moments*, 45.

We may witness the support we receive from family or friends or clergy, and conclude, "I am not alone. My grief may be personal and unique, but there are others who know how it feels."

When you say Kaddish or light a yahrzeit candle, when you attend a Yizkor service or a minyan at a house of mourning, you are doing something positive. More important, you are affirming that life is *something*—something to be cherished despite its brevity, something to be valued despite its pain, and something to be remembered despite the void of death. The answer to the question should be clear: *We are something! Our lives are something!* The bad news is that we are just dust and ashes. The good news—in fact, the best news of all—is that it was for our sake that the world was created. We are *not* nothing! We are, *definitely,* something!

ten

To Live a Thousand Years

During our Yizkor service on Yom Kippur, this paragraph and a congregational response totally fascinate me:

> If some messenger were to come to us with the offer that death should be overthrown, but with the one inseparable condition that birth should also cease; if the existing generation were given the chance to live for ever, but on the clear understanding that never again would there be a child, or youth, or first love, never again new persons with new hopes, new ideas, new achievements; ourselves for always and never any others—could the answer be in doubt? "We shall not fear the summons of death; we shall remember those who have gone before us, and those who will come after us!"[1]

Most people I know want to live as long as they can, and they wish the same for their family and friends. They are understandably sad when a loved one dies, and it seems like death comes too soon at whatever age it occurs. It is possible that a life of a thousand years would be great, but a life of one hundred years would be more realistic. We find the reference to a thousand years in Ps 90: "For in Your sight a thousand years are like yesterday that has

---

1. Stern, ed., *Gates of Repentance*, 484.

passed, like a watch of the night."[2] I think it's important to give some background about this psalm, to focus on the meaning of a thousand years, and to provide more realistic expectations for our lives.

In the Bible, Ps 90 consists of seventeen verses. Eight of those verses are found in our prayer book. The psalm is introduced in the Bible with the words "A prayer of Moses, the man of God."[3] Of the one hundred fifty psalms, seventy-three are directly attributed to King David. The Talmud contends that David included in the book quotations from so-called works of the elders such as Abraham, Solomon, and Moses. The great Jewish commentators of the Middle Ages—Rashi and ibn Ezra—believed that David couldn't have written all of the psalms, and many modern commentators and scholars agree with that viewpoint. As a matter of fact, a number of them seem to be from a period later than that of David. Of all the psalms, the ninetieth Psalm is the one that mentions Moses in the introduction.

The main theme of this psalm is the brevity of humanity and the eternity of God. In his commentary on Ps 90, Dr. A. Cohen wrote, "In sublime language it dwells upon the transitory character of man's existence, but in no pessimistic mood. If life is brief, its moments are precious and must not be wasted in vain pursuits. The swift passing of his stay upon earth would render it meaningless and purposeless, were it not that God is everlasting and in Him is man's abiding dwelling-place."[4] My own reading of the psalm leads me to conclude that Moses recognized that God has always existed and will continue to exist as a Creator and Protector. A long time for God is a short time for you and me—a thousand years are equivalent to a day. A "watch in the night" according to Israelite time was three hours. As short as that seems to us and seemed to them, it is like nothing for God. But Moses reasoned that it is not the quantity of our time that matters; it's the quality. So, it is incumbent upon us to use our time wisely. The alternative

2. Ps 90:4, *JPS Hebrew-English Tanakh*, 1527.
3. Ps 90:1, *JPS Hebrew-English Tanakh*, 1526.
4. Cohen, *Psalms*, 297.

is to feel as fragile as grass that grows and is cut down in a day. The psalmist ends by asking for the ability to understand God's ways and to use that understanding to make daily life meaningful.

This philosophy contradicts the idea of living for a thousand years, for the latter philosophy ascribes value to an exceptionally long life. Imagine if you were now in your thousandth year. You would have been born during the Geonim period of Jewish history, when the heads of the Talmudic academies of Babylonia were viewed as the spiritual leaders of the Jews, and you would have been a contemporary of the great Saadya Gaon, who introduced rationalism into the study of the Talmud and criticized the Karaite heretics. You would have been about seventy when Rashi was born, more than one hundred when the Crusades began, around two hundred fifty when the Magna Carta was signed, more than five hundred years old when Columbus discovered America and when the Jews were expelled from Spain. The list could go on and on. From a historical perspective, it would be fascinating to have lived through those times. But the actual prospect of living even half of the thousand years tends to boggle our minds. And, the details of what it would mean to physically live that long make it seem like pure fantasy.

Truth be told, to think about living a thousand years *is* pure fantasy. In a country in which the life expectancy of men is seventy-six and of women is eighty-one, even one hundred years seems fantastic rather than an average. It's a Jewish folk custom, more than a religious tradition, to wish someone a long life. In Hebrew, we say, *ahd meiah v'esreem*. And in Yiddish, it's *biz hundert und tzvantzik*. It means "to one hundred and twenty." It refers to the fact that Moses lived that long. But the wish is not merely a wish for the greatest quantity of all. Methusaleh and Noah, Abraham, Isaac, and Jacob were among those who lived longer than that age. It is, then, more realistic to expect—or, at least, to hope—to achieve a life of great quality more than a life of great quantity. We would all like to live as long as possible, and to be as healthy as possible for however many years it may be. We would have preferred that the loved ones or friends that we remember had lived longer. And, we would no doubt wish that a miracle cure would be discovered today, or at least in our lifetime, for all deadly diseases.

But if we only dwell on what could be, what could have been, and what we wish to be, we can become stuck in a world as full of fantasy as the idea of living for a thousand years. Moses—or whoever wrote Ps 90—had the right idea when he said, "Teach us to count our days rightly, that we may obtain a wise heart."[5] My interpretation of that line is that we should be wise enough to know that our days are what we make of them. If a day is going badly, think about how it could have been worse, or what you can learn from it, or how tomorrow can be better. If you receive bad news, think about how to cope with it instead of making it worse by being immobilized by self-pity and doubt. If you have developed a bad relationship with someone, think about ways to improve it instead of wasting your life by harboring resentment or hatred. If you are heartbroken that a loved one or friend has died and that you are no longer able to share your life with them, think about how the way you live your life can bring honor to their memory. In other words, think about what is positive, possible, and constructive. Don't become neutralized or take a step backward by dwelling on what is negative, impossible, and destructive. We must all face the fact that there are days that we no longer have and may never have. And, there are days that we can have and will have. It's all within our control to have hope and faith.

To want to live a thousand years is indeed a fantasy, and some would call it selfish—especially if it meant that no one else would be born. To make each day a blessing can be our reality, an attitude that can enrich our lives and the lives of others, and bring honor to the memory of our loved ones.

5. Ps 90:12, *JPS Hebrew-English Tanakh*, 1527.

eleven

The Freedom to Remember

If I were to ask you to join in a word-association game with the word *Passover*, you would probably respond with a variety of answers. Included might be "seder" or "matzah" or "company" or "haggadah"—or any of a number of other words. I'd probably come up with some of those, too. And, I would add the words "freedom" and "remember." "Freedom," because it is the main theme of the holiday, as it is reflected in our prayer book liturgy and in what we say and do at the seder. "Remember," because it conveys the purpose of the holiday, a sense that there is no way we can observe Passover and let it come to a conclusion without remembering.

It is these two words that come to mind at a Yizkor service for Passover or for the other three holidays on which we observe Yizkor. At a Passover Yizkor service in particular, we are expected to remember, and to emphasize our freedom to do so. There are, essentially, five different names in Hebrew for the holiday we know as Passover—names that have been developed over the centuries since biblical times. Although the Exodus occurred more than 3,200 years ago, the name of Passover as *Z'man Cheiruteinu* (Season of Our Freedom) is probably about half that old. The name appears once in the Haggadah—in the *Kiddush* (wine blessing) near the beginning. It appears as well in one of the prayers we read during the service. And even when that particular phrase is not

used, there is an undeniable message on Passover of the importance of freedom—for those who left slavery behind in Egypt, for
us today, and for our Jewish and non-Jewish brothers and sisters
all over the world.

By the same token, remembering is clearly a priority for Passover. As it says at the beginning of the Haggadah: "We assemble in
fulfillment of the mitzvah: 'Remember the day on which you went
forth from Egypt, from the house of bondage, and how God freed
you with a mighty hand.'"[1] That quotation from the thirteenth
chapter of Exodus sets the tone for the occasion. As we proceed
through the narration, we remember what happened to our ancestors—and the words "our ancestors" in this case applies to Jews,
Christians, and Muslims. Later, we are urged to feel "as though we
ourselves had gone forth from Egypt."[2] That mandate should motivate us to be concerned with the stranger and the less fortunate in
our own society, to be empathetic and not just sympathetic. So, we
are encouraged to remember not merely as an intellectual exercise,
but also to feel as we remember and to do because we remember.

The purpose of a Yizkor service, of lighting a yahrzeit candle,
and of saying prayers like the Kaddish is to remember our loved
ones who have died and to show honor and respect for their memory by these conscious and sacred acts. We have the freedom to
remember who we want and how we want to do it. While we may
do so in memory of a parent or (God forbid) a child, a spouse or a
sibling, a grandparent or other relative, we are also free—as far as
Reform Judaism is concerned—to be involved in the sacred act of
remembering friends or even to honor the memory of those who
died in the Holocaust, those for whom no one is left to remember
them. And, we have the freedom to remember what we want no
matter how religious we may be or may not be. Our memories of
those who have died can be very selective or all-inclusive. We may
recall someone's greatest achievements and qualities, and seek to
aspire to them. Or, we may remember their worst habits and flaws,
and seek to avoid them. We may think of a special person and what

1. Bronstein, *Passover Haggadah*, 21.
2. Ibid., 56.

he or she meant to us, and have that act of remembering bring joyful tears to our eyes. Or, we may recollect an important event or a certain moment, and be tempted to laugh—even when we think we shouldn't.

At times throughout the year we are reminded of our link with the history of the Jewish people, but it is rarely so prominent as it is on Passover. Similarly, there may be times throughout the year when we are reminded of a loved one who has died, but the occasions of Yizkor remind us of how much our own personal history was affected by those we recall. As one of the readings in our previous prayer book said, "those who live no more, echo still within our thoughts and words, and what they did is part of what we have become."[3]

The seder liturgy mentions times when the Jewish people were objects of distrust and victims of surveillance, times when it was risky to even have a seder. That applies specifically to the Middle Ages when the blood libel accusation was so prevalent, but it could apply to certain countries in the twentieth and twenty-first centuries too. It became so dangerous for Jews to have seders in the former Soviet Union that there were many Jews who were not aware of what a seder was and what it meant. The mass emigration of Jews from the former Soviet Union to Israel and North America near the end of the twentieth century occurred for those who became observant and those who did not, but even the least observant came to know what a seder signified. So, we who live in freedom are urged to cherish that freedom that God gave to our ancestors and not take our good fortune for granted.

Parallel to this is our freedom to remember our loved ones who have died. No one can tell us that we are not allowed to remember them. No one can prohibit us from remembering so overtly, from actually going beyond the intellectual exercise in our own minds and coming to a service to share an emotional and spiritual bond with others. That is one thing that freedom does for us. It makes us more aware of the world around us and affords us more opportunities. When you participate in a community, you

3. Stern, ed., *Gates of Prayer*, 625.

are reminded that you are not the only mourner around, and that remembering our dead is both an individual and a communal mitzvah. Remembering can make us sad, but it can also give us strength. Being a mourner can make us feel isolated, but being with other mourners can make us feel that we belong, and that we have support.

No matter how many times you mourn, you are using your freedom to remember. When that happens, you are taking the opportunity to pause in the midst of your busy life, to go beyond the realm of your individual world, and to join together with a community of mourners. In so doing, you are engaging in the mitzvah of remembering and you are bringing the greatest respect possible to the memories of your loved ones. May we each always cherish our freedom to remember. And may we use the opportunities available to us to solidify our links with those who have died and with our fellow mourners, who form a very special and a very sacred community.

twelve

What We Can Learn from Death

"What we can learn from death." Notice the way this title is phrased. It's not a question. It's a statement, positive and assertive. And it's an anticipatory clause, too—the kind that could have a colon following it and then a list. It's a hopeful clause, offered as a means of finding value and worth in an experience that may cause us to question the value of life and of ourselves. It's what you would expect from Judaism, a religion that promotes the belief that if life can present us with opportunities for learning, so can death. It's something you would and should expect from a rabbi who, in dealing with the anticipation and reality of death and ceremonies and rituals following it, believes that from death much can be learned and applied to our lives. What we can learn from death fits into three categories: the emotional, the communal, and the philosophical.

There is no denying that death produces emotions, usually those tied in with grief. Death can make us sad, worried, angry, and depressed. When a death is prolonged and full of suffering, its occurrence can make us feel relieved. When we are *not* there when the person dies, we may feel guilty. When we *are* there, we may feel fortunate. Psychological insights have indicated that we should be encouraged to express our emotions about death, that crying is acceptable and suppressing our feelings is not. Confronting our emotions is advised, denying them is discouraged.

We can learn from death the emotional qualities of courage and compassion. Among those who mourn are people whose loved ones showed extraordinary courage in the face of serious illness and death. Even in dealing with the uncertainty of what happens after death, they were able to help make decisions. Some mourners have exhibited great courage in making decisions and in reconciling themselves with their loved one's death. It took courage to help them deal with what can be uncertain and vague as well as with what can be fearsome and overwhelming. At times when we are most vulnerable, we need to find the courage and resolve to move on and to move forward.

We can also learn compassion from death. The ability to feel for another person is one of the gifts with which human beings are endowed. It can be reflected in wanting to help a loved one who is seriously ill or in being willing to let them go. It can be reflected in doing what we can to make them comfortable or in listening to their expression of wishes. Compassion can also be apparent in the case of a sudden death, when others volunteer to lend a hand, to provide a shoulder to cry on, to be there without saying a word, or to do something before they are asked. We can learn compassion from death in the hard work of doctors and nurses and paramedics and ambulance drivers who weep with you when your loved one dies. We can learn compassion from death when we have had the chance to talk with the person who is dying, and he or she is more concerned about how we are and will be than about how they feel.

The second category is the communal. Whenever you choose to share your grief with others—in conversation, at a service, or through social media—you are linking yourself with a community. No matter whether the death of the person you mourn was sudden or prolonged, from a disease or an accident, a welcome relief after suffering or a tragedy that ended a life too soon, you have something in common with others. We can learn from death that there is support for us. Although the person we mourn was unique, others know what it is like for a child to die or for a parent to be confined to a nursing home. There are others whose loved ones are dead because of cancer or heart attacks or traffic accidents. In the last couple decades, we have come to see the growing influence of support groups that are formally organized by therapists or other health professionals and are held in hospitals, churches, or synagogues. Support groups can include those we already know or people we do not know who show compassion by uniting for a common purpose. They are there to say that they know what we are going through, that we are not alone, and that they want to help.

And, linked with these expressions of compassion at the time of death or shortly thereafter is a true sense of community. In Judaism, we have always emphasized the gathering of the community at the time of a death—for the funeral itself and immediately after, for minyan services, for saying Kaddish at services, and for observing yahrzeits. You can mourn at home, you can go away and contemplate what your loved one meant to you, or you can isolate yourself and believe that you will never recover. But we are offered the opportunities to connect, to express grief, to mourn, and to begin the process of healing and recovery as individuals within the context of the community. And we are urged to keep alive the memories of our loved ones in a public way—by having children named after them in a public or private ceremony, by the unveiling of a tombstone at the cemetery, by making a donation to the synagogue, or by establishing a fund in memory of the deceased.

The third category is the philosophical. Both the funeral service and the prayers in our prayer book deal with the reality of death and the meaning we can derive from it. In the funeral service, we hear these words: "The dust returns to the earth as it was; the spirit returns to God who gave it. It is only the house of the spirit which we now lay within the earth; the spirit itself cannot die."[1] We are encouraged to believe that the soul, the spirit, lives on in many ways.

One philosophical lesson we can learn from death is the value of life. A meditation in *Gates of Prayer* begins: "Judaism teaches us to understand death as part of the Divine pattern of the universe.

1. Goor, *For Sacred Moments*, 45.

Actually, we could not have our sensitivity without fragility."² Another reminds us that "we do best homage to our dead when we live our lives most fully, even in the shadow of our loss. For each of our lives is worth the life of the whole world; in each one is the breath of the Ultimate One."³ These expressions are typical of the Jewish belief that death is natural, and that it is important for us to live our lives, not only for our own well-being, but also because our loved ones who have died would have wanted the same for us.

And we can learn from death the need for a sense of perspective. Those who experience a relative's sudden death sometimes are grateful that there was not a lot of suffering. Those who watch a relative die slowly and painfully may wish that it would have happened quickly. Some people live for too long a time and others for too short a time, and we may feel either way because of our own experiences and beliefs. But death can help us put things in perspective. Again, one of our prayer book readings is worth considering: "The contemplation of death should plant within the soul elevation and peace. Above all, it should make us see things in their true light. For all things which seem foolish in the light of death are really foolish in themselves."⁴ It is this lesson that I have learned over the years—to take the opportunity to say what you mean, to spend quality time when you can, to resolve problems quickly and amicably, to not be offended so easily, and to worry about what you can't control less frequently. Too many people die without learning and applying such lessons while they are alive. Too many people live with fear and anger, regret and worry, foolishness and falsehoods. They need a sense of perspective, and to gain it because of a death is better than to have not gained it at all.

What we can learn from death can affect our lives—their quality and, to a certain extent, their quantity. Health care professionals tell us that people with positive outlooks live longer than those with negative outlooks. With courage and compassion, with support and a sense of community, by valuing life and maintaining

2. Stern, ed., *Gates of Prayer*, 625.
3. Ibid.
4. Ibid. 623.

a sense of perspective, we can make death more than a final fare-well. Together, these qualities can help us not only to face the future with hope and strength but also to shape it with promise and faith.

thirteen

Does God Remember?

The Yizkor service is a unique Jewish experience. Tradition prescribes that it be held four times a year—on Yom Kippur, Shemini Atzeret, Pesach, and Shavuot. It is only on Yom Kippur that it isn't really part of another service, and it is for some Jews the only service they attend during the year. The prayers are special, too, concentrating on one basic theme rather than several—death, and how it relates to life. For me, the most interesting of the prayers is the one the first word of which has become the popular name of the service, more properly called *Hazkarat Neshamot* (the Mentioning/Remembering of Souls). It is this prayer that begins with the words *Yizkor Elohim* (May God remember).

For the modern Jew, those words can be problematic. Human beings remember, but what does it say about our theology if we accept the idea that God "remembers"? Does God do other human activities too? If God has a memory, does God also make use of the senses like human beings do? Our ancestors firmly believed in God's ability to relate to human beings in ways that human beings could understand. If God created us in God's "image," they reasoned, God was certainly capable of being an extension of ourselves, capable of doing what human beings do but doing it better. They envisioned God as true perfection, omniscient, omnipotent, and omnipresent. God was, for them, the epitome of good, love, righteousness, and justice. And, as perfect as God was, as superhuman—or, more correctly—*supra*human, they could describe God only in human terms, such as Father, Lord, Master, or Creator, among others. No language I am aware of has developed a separate vocabulary for God. And so, when the Maccabees composed the Yizkor prayer to mourn their deceased comrades, they asked that God remember those people. If you know that the Hebrew word *Maccabee* is an acrostic for the biblical phrase *Mee Chamocha Baeilim Adonai* (Who is like You among the gods, YHWH), then you shouldn't be surprised that they ascribed memory to God.

Such anthropomorphism (describing God in human terms) may have been comfortable for the Maccabees, but it isn't so comfortable for most Jews today. We think that we tend to intellectualize more about God than our ancestors did, although we aren't necessarily more intellectual or more rational than they were. We simply are more concerned about being more rational than emotional when it comes to God. Acknowledging a difference in how we view the world and God's role in it as compared to how our ancestors did more than two thousand years ago, we approach their views and words with our own understanding and interpretation.

For many of us it is incomprehensible that God wrote the Torah. We might say that divinely inspired human beings wrote it down after sustaining an oral tradition for many centuries. In Exodus, we read about God appearing in a burning bush, hardening Pharaoh's heart, causing the plagues to occur, and dividing the Sea of Reeds. We may tend not to accept any of these miracles literally because they contradict our theology. Instead, we explain them in terms that we can accept and understand, perhaps through a scientific explanation or a metaphorical interpretation. In that way I don't think that we are much different than our ancestors. We just accept and understand God in different terms and on different levels.

Amid all of this talk about God, though, it is easy to ignore the main point of our prayers and of our services: in asking God to "remember," we are, ourselves, remembering. We are reaching out with hope and faith that we want to partner with God in honoring our loved ones who have died. Whether it is on a special occasion or on a daily basis, we can show our love by remembering. Our love did not end when their lives ended, and it survives as long as our memories of them survive. To remember is not that difficult, but to take it a step further and to join with other people in remembering is incredible. Some might regard that step as an obligation or a responsibility, but I regard it as an opportunity. It is an opportunity not to wallow in our grief and commiserate with other people doing the same thing, but to affirm our faith that love overcomes death because our memories constitute a positive and uplifting aspect of our lives. And when we derive emotional support from our peers and share the experience of remembering, we are doing what God does and wants us to do.

Does God remember? I think so. And I think God sees us remembering and hears us praying and serves as a source of strength for us, and smiles at what we are doing. That may sound terribly anthropomorphic, but I believe that God cares about what we do just as any good parent would. When we remember actively, when we affirm life and love, when we form a holy community, we draw closer to God and to one another. May the memories of your loved ones always be for a blessing, and may you always be blessed by remembering them just as God does.

fourteen

Death and Regrets

Consider the following exchange, which occurred at a Jewish funeral. After the service, everyone left the cemetery except for the mourning husband and the rabbi. The husband remained at the grave for a long while; finally, the rabbi approached him. 'The service is long over, it is time for you to leave," he said. The man waved him away. 'You don't understand. I loved my wife." "I am sure you did," the rabbi answered, "but you have been here a very long time. You should go now." Again the husband said, "You don't understand. I loved my wife." Once more the rabbi urged him to leave. "But you don't understand," the man told him. "I loved my wife—and once, I almost told her."[1]

This story from Rabbi Joseph Telushkin's book *Words That Hurt, Words That Heal* is both touching and true. To be able to say "I love you" to someone is one of the greatest things we can do. To be unable to say those three words can deprive someone of a sense that they are valued and important. And when death has prevented us from saying what we never said, or from saying again what we had always said, the impact can potentially be devastating. Death and regrets sometimes go hand in hand. And we need

1. Telushkin, *Words That Hurt, Words That Heal*, 154.

to understand about how natural it is to feel regret, how we have to try to get past regret, and how we can replace that feeling with another, better feeling.

It is said that whenever someone dies, it is too soon. In the ideal world that some people create, they hope that their loved ones will live just short of forever—short enough to not become a burden, long enough to share all of the good experiences and special occasions we want them to share. The depth of our relationship with them urges us to wish on some level that everything will be fine with them all of the time. If we have a problem with someone, we'll take care of it eventually. If we say something wrong or mean, we can apologize for it later. If they do something mean or terrible to us, there will be plenty of time for them to make it up to us.

Yet, when those people die with their work unfinished and conflicts unresolved, with words left unsaid and apologies never made, it is natural for their survivors to feel regret and experience guilt. If only it had been different, their death would not be so tragic. If I had made a different decision, he would still be here. If I had been nicer, she would still be alive. In the face of death, our imagined scenarios of what could have been and should have been but never came to be can vault us into a cycle of regret. It is natural for us to wish that what happened did not happen, and for us to believe that we alone had the power to make things better, and that if we had used that power wisely, the person would still be alive.

I have told many of my congregants that we don't have the power to change the fact that a relative or friend has died. We do not have the power to change the way that they died, or the circumstances that led up to the death, or the previous decisions and choices that may ultimately have helped bring about their death. However, we do have the power to decide how we will react to the fact that the person has died. We might have a "gut reaction"—an instinctive, automatic, emotional response, like crying. For no apparent reason, we may be moved to tears. Or, tears may be triggered by a memory that makes us sad because it is the memory itself, and because it is only a memory. We might also have a clear and lucid reaction, we might be reasonable without being cold, and we might be realistic without being heartless: "The person I loved has died and there is nothing that will change that. He would want me to go on with my life. I need to pull myself together. I need to help the rest of my family."

In her book *How to Go On Living When Someone You Love Dies*, Therese A. Rando wrote:

> The third series of processes necessary for successful accommodation and resolution of grief focuses on your moving into your new life, that is, life without your deceased loved one, without forgetting your old life. This involves: 1. Developing a new relationship with the deceased. 2. Keeping your loved one "alive" appropriately. 3. Forming a new identity based on your being without this person and encompassing the changes you have made to adjust to his death. 4. Taking the freed-up emotional energy that used to be invested in your loved one and reinvesting it in other relationships, objects, activities, roles, and hopes that can offer emotional satisfaction back to you.[2]

All of these perspectives and activities can get us past regret, but they have to get us to more than a new, busy schedule that blurs our eyes, tires our bodies, and dulls our emotions. The better feelings that we need to replace regret are the feelings of thankfulness and appreciation.

The idea of thankfulness when we think about death may seem to be inappropriate and out of place. On the contrary, it is *very* appropriate. We often take for granted the fact that people have lived at all, that they did what they did, and that we were privileged enough to know them, to love them, and to be affected by them. God forbid it should take a well-written and well-delivered eulogy to be the only catalyst to remind us what a great person someone was. To be thankful that your loved one or friend who has died lived a life that included you and brought you love and touched you is wonderful. That we can give thanks for the life of

2. Rando, *How to Go on Living*, 232.

our loved one should motivate us for a future without that person's physical presence but with the person's spiritual presence.

In addition to the feeling of thankfulness, the second feeling to nurture in the face of death is what I call appreciation. This is inherent in our Jewish tradition in the form of our many prayers and blessings. Our continual appreciation of our loved ones and friends who have died is shown by our lighting of yahrzeit candles and other customs so prevalent in our tradition. They are active examples of our sadness that someone has died and of our happiness that they lived. Ultimately we show through our tradition our appreciation not only of our loved ones and friends but also of the Source of all life, not only of our memories, but also of God. And when we do that, we strengthen ourselves. When we relate to God as Friend and Comforter and Sustainer, instead of God as Enemy and Bully and Executioner, then we can achieve a healing that protects us from the potential deep-seated pain that death can inflict on our very souls.

And our physical separation from those we have loved, our ending of time that we have spent with them, can give us a sense of appreciation for what we have and for who is still here with us. The psalmist, the ancient rabbis, modern rabbis, contemporary psychologists, and grief counselors all agree that grieving and returning to life gradually is a process. It is a process through which we move at different speeds and in different ways. The goal is to return to life without forgetting who has died, sustaining that person's memory and sustaining ourselves as well. We who have known love and have lost one who gave love to us need to appreciate love and keep love alive for ourselves and for others. We who would have liked to have more time with the person who died need to appreciate the time we have, to use it wisely and well, and to refrain from feelings of regret about what we feel could have been. We who have been touched by death need to affirm life, to appreciate the distinction between major and minor issues, and to devote our time to healing ourselves and others rather than regretting what was never said and what never came to be.

And so, knowing that it is natural to have regrets about death, let us work hard to get past them. Let us endeavor to accept the realities of death and the possibilities of life. Let us seek to develop a sense of thankfulness and appreciation, aware that life is a gift the quality of which *we* can determine. May we do so with God's help, with the support of those who love us and care for us, and with our own sense that we can determine what life will be like in the face of death.

fifteen

The Pain of Losing a Child: In Newtown and among Ourselves

A number of years ago, one of the families in my congregation in Hingham, Massachusetts, learned that their middle child—a cute little eight-year-old girl named Jennifer—had cancer. Her parents took different approaches to the news, and her older and younger brothers were also as different from one another as their parents. From that point on, the mother was a "tiger mom"—aggressive in her pursuit of answers, assertive in the presence of doctors and nurses, and optimistic in front of her daughter. The father maintained a steady and steely presence, keeping his nose to the grindstone as the breadwinner who had to keep working in order to have the health insurance that would pay for the enormous bills. What followed the diagnosis was a three-year period of ups and downs, hope and despair, that culminated in this beautiful child's death—less than a week before her older brother's bar mitzvah service. The funeral took place on Tuesday, shiva continued through Friday morning, and the bar mitzvah service and luncheon occurred on Shabbat while shiva resumed on Sunday. You may judge them, and maybe me, harshly as you read this, but it was what was best for that family at that time.

During the three years that this girl was hospitalized, I visited her frequently—both in Boston and in New York City. I remember clearly that when I would come home at night, I made a point of going upstairs, watching my five-year-old daughter sleep, praying to God on the girl's behalf, and thanking God that my daughter was safe and well. The parents separated and divorced not long after the death of their child, like some other parents who cannot handle the combination of anger and blame when a child dies. One good thing that happened was that our congregation established a fund in her memory, dedicated to providing scholarships for students to go to Israel—what this wonderful child would have done had she lived.

Some say that nothing is worse than the death of a child, and I can tell you that I have seen the enduring pain a child's loss has caused among my family, my friends, and my congregants. It seems unnatural and so wrong for a child to die before a parent—no matter how old the child may be. Some say that you can't really feel the pain of a child's death unless you are a parent, but I disagree. I have known many people who have no children but are deeply affected by the death of a child—people whose compassion and empathy are so essential to the healing of the parents. That has been amazingly obvious during the past week. You don't have to be a parent to mourn the deaths of twenty children and six adults in Newtown, Connecticut—six adults, each of whom was, of course, someone's child. You may relate to it differently as a parent than someone would who is not a parent, and you may relate to it in a special way as a teacher because school staff members were killed, and because the murders occurred in a school. What unites all of us who feel anger, sadness, despair, or frustration is a sense of what could have been if these children had lived. What we have in common is a belief that no one should be so evil, that innocent children should not be victimized, that the availability of guns is terrible, and that our mental health system must be changed. It is not my intention to focus only on the sorrow. Much more can and must be done.

This is not the first time that children have been mourned. The entire Joseph story in the Torah is predicated on Jacob being convinced that his favorite, beloved son is dead, and that he will never recover from this loss. Although a prolific family man,

Jacob is not really happy until his twelfth child—Joseph—is born. Rachel says, "God has taken away my disgrace,"[1] and she names the boy *Yosayf*, meaning, "May the Lord add another son for me."[2] Sure enough, she has another son. Then, as she is dying, she names him *Ben-oni*—"son of my suffering," but Jacob changes his name to *Binyamin*—"son of the right hand."[3]

The Torah tells us later that "Israel loved Joseph best of all his sons, for he was the child of his old age; and he had made him an ornamented tunic. And when his brothers saw that their father loved him more than any of his brothers, they hated him so that they could not speak a friendly word to him."[4] Reuben prevents him from being killed, and Judah suggests that he be sold to the Ishmaelites on their way to Egypt. When Joseph's tunic with blood on it is taken to Jacob, he reacts immediately and cries out, "My son's tunic! A savage beast devoured him! Joseph was torn by a beast!"[5] He then tears his clothes, puts on sackcloth, mourns for his son many days, refuses to be comforted, and says, "I will go down mourning to my son in Sheol,"[6] meaning that the death of his beloved son is going to be the death of him.

Thirteen years later there is a famine in Canaan, and Jacob sends all his sons except Benjamin to Egypt (since he fears that "Benjamin might meet with disaster"[7]) to buy food. Joseph, who has become Pharaoh's second-in-command unbeknownst to his brothers, recognizes them and takes Simeon hostage, ordering the brothers to bring their youngest brother down to Egypt when they return for more food. When he is told of this, Jacob replies: "It is always me that you bereave; Joseph is no more and Simeon is no more, and now you would take away Benjamin. These things

---

1. Gen 30:23, *JPS Hebrew-English Tanakh*, 61

2. Gen 30:24, 61.

3. Gen 35:18, 74.

4. Gen 37: 3–4, 77.

5. Gen 37:33, 79.

6. Gen 37:35, 79.

7. Gen 42:4, 89.

always happen to me!"[8] Although Reuben makes an offer to his father to protect Benjamin in exchange for the lives of Reuben's two sons, Jacob refuses his offer, saying, "my son must not go down with you, for his brother is dead and he alone is left. If he meets with disaster on the journey you are taking, you will send my white head down to Sheol in grief."[9] Judah promises to take care of Benjamin, and Jacob gives in, saying, "If I am to be bereaved, I shall be bereaved."[10] The brothers appear again before Joseph, the anonymous Egyptian official, but Joseph recognizes Benjamin and hides his emotions. He arranges to have a goblet put in with the food he gives them and then accuses them of stealing. At this point Judah approaches Joseph. Eventually, unlike the parents of the children killed in Newtown, Jacob is reunited with his favorite son and even gets to meet and bless his grandchildren.

Although it is not my intention to think only about the sorrow, it must be recognized. What happened in Newtown has made some of us sad, angry, and hopeless. President Obama mentioned that this was the fourth time in his tenure that he had gone to comfort the victims of mass murderers. We cannot exactly understand the depth of the sorrow of parents, siblings, uncles and aunts, cousins and grandparents unless we have experienced it ourselves. But we can project our own feelings onto this situation and personalize it, as I did with my daughter and the girl in my congregation. We can wish that this never happened or that Adam Lanza had never been born, that his mother had never bought guns or that Lanza had been institutionalized, that God had intervened and stopped him from this heinous act, or that a highly trained security guard had killed him before he killed others. None of those scenarios came to be or will come to be. Like many tragedies in our lives, like many situations or events that make us sad or angry, the question is how we react to it. The question is whether we are any different now than we were before. The question is, will it help to know why

---

8. Gen 42:36, 92.
9. Gen 42:38, 92.
10. Gen 43:14, 93.

it happened, and will we learn anything from that knowledge, and will we do anything about it?

If you read Liza Long's article "I Am Adam Lanza's Mother," you are aware that our mental health system is not where it needs to be. She concludes with these words:

> No one wants to send a 13-year old genius who loves Harry Potter and his snuggle animal collection to jail. But our society, with its stigma on mental illness and its broken healthcare system, does not provide us with other options. Then another tortured soul shoots up a fast food restaurant. A mall. A kindergarten classroom. And we wring our hands and say, "Something must be done." I agree that something must be done. It's time for a meaningful, nation-wide conversation about mental health. That's the only way our nation can ever truly heal."[11]

Just as something must be done about guns and mental health in this country, something must be done by and for parents who have experienced the death of a child. To do nothing, to act as if nothing happened, or to become frozen in the time before the sadness is not healthy. To be angry but to have no positive outlet for the anger, to ask questions the answers to which we really don't want to hear, and to think that we are alone with our feelings are not productive. We need a framework for action, and here it is: In the book of Leviticus, the Holiness Code urges us to behave as God would want us to behave: "You shall not pick your vineyard bare, or gather the fallen fruit of your vineyard; you shall leave them for the poor and the stranger."[12] "You shall not defraud your fellow."[13] "Do not favor the poor or show deference to the rich"[14] "Do not deal basely with your countrymen. Do not profit by the blood of your neighbor."[15] "Love your fellow as yourself."[16] All of this

11. Long, "I Am Adam Lanza's Mother."

12. Lev 19: 10, 251

13. Lev 19: 13, 251

14. Lev 19: 15, 251

15. Lev 19:16, 252

16. Lev 19:18, 252

involves engaging in *tikkun olam*—picking up the broken pieces of our world one at a time and helping to repair the world with each positive act of valuing life, identifying with others, and showing them kindness and love. *This is what I have to do. I cannot sit and wallow in the sorrow.* I cannot continue to be mesmerized by the coverage of this tragedy from every angle and do nothing. And I would hope that the parents of children who have died would feel the same way.

That is why we asked for healing for the parents and teachers and community of Newtown at our service last Friday, and why, at last Saturday's bar mitzvah service, we acknowledged the absence of an aunt, uncle, and cousins from Newtown. That is why I discussed the Reform Movement's position on gun control with my postconfirmation class on Sunday, and why we had a brief service on Sunday. That is why I have signed petitions this week and brainstormed with my fellow Three Village clergy about what we could do together. That is why I participated in a conference call yesterday and e-mailed the president and our senators and congressional representative. That is why I have decided to participate in the nationwide interreligious Sabbath to end gun violence in two weeks and asked the Social Action Committee to put on their agenda some type of educational program or activity. And that is why I will continue to be active; because I believe that we are not alone unless we want to be, that we must be the angels to cancel out the devils in our midst, and that every single kind word and every single generous act and every single unselfish deed can all make a positive difference for us and others.

What can you do? If you are inclined to get angry quickly, stop and think before doing so. If you are always blaming others for your sadness, look into your own soul. If you hold a grudge, stop it. If you seek vengeance, give it up. If you love to sabotage, find something else to love. You and I are not powerless. We give a victory to the Adam Lanzas of the world if we think we are powerless, if we wallow in our despair, and if we do nothing positive. *That is not what God wants us to do, that is not what Judaism urges us to do, and that is not what you should want yourself to do.*

And what about parents whose child has died? Their world is broken, their hopes are shattered, their hearts are torn, and their dreams may have vanished. But, they can choose to be like John Walsh, whose son Adam was murdered in 1981, and who created *America's Most Wanted* and *The Hunt with John Walsh* to help other families who experienced tragedies. Or they could be like Sherri Mandell, whose son Koby was murdered in 2001, who established the Koby Mandell Foundation to help and inspire other parents, and who wrote *The Blessing of a Broken Heart: The Journey of Healing from Horrific Grief*—a truly moving book. Parents who experience tragedies may not be able to completely put their world back the way it was. But, in the spirit of *tikkun olam* (repair of the world), it can be done to repair themselves one step at a time, piece by piece, to create a new reality, a new normal. Parents do not have to be or feel powerless or alone. They can accept the empathy shown toward them, and share their own empathy with others. This is what God would want them to do, and what their children would want them to do.

My daughter, that little girl I used to check on, is now a married woman. She keeps a blog, and she concluded this week's entry with these words: "If we want to honor the memories of those gone too soon, we need to bring more love into this world. I'm not so naive as to think that love can solve all, but I know that a little can go a long way. So, please, give more hugs. Truly be there for people, not out of obligation or routine, but because you want to be. Ask how they are, and don't just wait to hear the answer, but listen to what they're really saying."[17]

She is as idealistic as ever, and I think that's good. Sometimes we ignore those who are too quiet and pay attention to those who are too loud. We need to strike a balance in our lives, and we need to start now. If not now, when? The fund established in memory of Jennifer, my eight-year-old congregant who died of cancer, took many children to Israel to experience "the best summer of my life." Although she was a tragic victim of what was, and a mere glimpse

17. Tananbaum, *Life Is Like a Box of Chocolates* (blog), December 2012 post.

of what could have been, her death motivated others to appreciate and enrich their lives. The pain of losing a child or an adult can scar us permanently, but we can bring meaning to our lives by how we choose to live despite the pain. Join with me locally and with others nationally as we do exactly that.

sixteen

The Mystery of the Kaddish

Its origin is mysterious. We find foreshadowings of it in the Biblical books; prayers for the dead are mentioned in the Books of Maccabees; snatches of the Kaddish reach us in the legends of Talmudic teachers; and echoes of it in the writings of the early Mystics: but the Prayer in its entirety we find neither in the Bible, nor in the Mishna, nor in the vast Talmudic and Midrashic literatures. It seems to be a gradual growth, continued from generation to generation, from age to age, until in the period of the *Gaonim*, some twelve centuries ago, it attained the form which we have before us in our Prayer Books.[1]

This is the description of the Kaddish prayer, written by the great Rabbi Joseph H. Hertz in his annotated traditional prayer book. The Kaddish is one of the most well-known, important, and mysterious prayers for Jews, and it is especially significant for anyone who recites it in a synagogue, at home, or in the cemetery. It is simultaneously general and specific—general if we join with other mourners, and specific if we say it while remembering a relative or a friend. Most Jews, regardless of the amount of Hebrew training they have had, can say the Kaddish. Written in Aramaic—an ancient language that looks like Hebrew—the prayer

1. Hertz, *Authorized Daily Prayer Book*, 270.

71

can be read in those characters or in English transliteration, from a card or a book or by heart. What is it about the Kaddish that makes it so special and, in a way, so mysterious?

First of all, we need a little background information. There are actually five versions of the Kaddish in Jewish tradition, two of which appear in our prayer book. One is called the *Chatzi Kaddish*, meaning the "Half-Kaddish" but it is popularly referred to as the Reader's Kaddish because the service leader says the prayer out loud with occasional responses from the congregation. The *Chatzi Kaddish* is chanted prior to the *Bar'chu* and functions as a bridge between the preliminary prayers and the main section of the liturgy. By its very nature, the Kaddish is a doxology, a praise of God, and it was said to mark the end of a period of study of religious texts. Written in Aramaic—the vernacular of our people following the Babylonian exile—it was used at first in academies of learning. The teacher would dismiss his students with this prayer, which praises God and expresses the Messianic hope that God's kingdom will be established on earth.

The other version in our prayer book is what we know as the Mourner's Kaddish. In Hebrew, it's called *Kaddish Yatom*, or "Orphan's Kaddish." It is two lines longer than the *Chatzi Kaddish*, the last two lines to be specific, and it always appears after the *Aleinu* in the final section of the service. Of those two lines, the next-to-last one is in Aramaic like the rest of the prayer. But, the last line is in Hebrew, and is a quotation from the book of Job. Do these additional lines automatically change the Kaddish from a scholar's prayer to a mourner's prayer? Not really, at least not on the surface.

Apparently, the Kaddish used to have a line at the beginning that mentioned the traditional belief in the resurrection of the dead when the Messiah comes. Historians believe that the Kaddish became a prayer for mourners in Germany in the thirteenth century as a result of persecution by the Crusaders. It is part of the mystery of the Kaddish that the time and reason for the elimination of that line are unknown. And the other mysterious aspect of the Kaddish is why we say it in memory of someone when it never mentions death. Why do we say a prayer the name of which means "holy," a prayer that contains eight consecutive adjectives conveying positive feelings about God, at a time when praising God might not be uppermost in our minds?

The answer can be given in one word—acceptance. Judaism is a religion that encourages mourners to accept the reality of a death as soon as possible. That acceptance is to be exemplified in word with the Kaddish and in deed with our mourning customs. The words themselves don't actually tell the mourner to face the facts and accept reality. They simply praise God, express the Messianic hope, and ask for the blessings of life and peace. The acceptance, then, is implicit. The Kaddish is not a tribute of blind loyalty to God, as some would say, because it heaps praise on God. It is acceptance of God's role as the Ruler of a world in which life and death occur. It is not a prayer that either glorifies or condemns death. It is a prayer that affirms that life is a gift not to be taken for granted. It is not a prayer in which we ask or demand of God that no one die. It is a prayer that reminds the living to have faith and hope.

Above all, when we say the Kaddish, we are thanking God for having created the person or persons we remember and honor as we recite the prayer. In praising the Source of Life, we acknowledge the value of life. We affirm how much our loved one's life meant to us, how important it is to recognize the fact of that person's death, accept it, and move on with our own lives. And the Kaddish is a prayer designed to be said in public, in a group, as part of a congregation. The mourner who lights a yahrzeit candle at home alone is engaged in a wonderful mitzvah. But an added depth and meaning come to reciting the Kaddish when you do so in the presence of other people who have feelings profoundly similar to your own. It is helpful and even comforting to know and to see that you are not the only person expressing grief caused by death. And it's beautiful to know that neither death nor the grief that follows it is unnatural.

In his classic work, *The Jewish Way in Death and Mourning,* Maurice Lamm wrote: "The Kaddish serves as an epilogue to human life as, historically, it served as an epilogue to Torah study

. . . [it] is a spiritual handclasp between the generations, one that connects two lifetimes."[2]

The connection of which Lamm speaks will never disappear as long as Jews recite the Kaddish. Death is mysterious, but the strength of love and faith and hope affirmed by the Kaddish do not have to be a mystery to any of us. May this prayer always have tremendous meaning, bring us consolation, and affirm the importance of a love that cannot die, a person that cannot be forgotten, and a life that we can live that is both happy and long.

2. Lamm, *Jewish Way*, 158.

Bibliography

Ain, Meryl et al., eds. *The Living Memories Project: Legacies That Last*. Milford, OH: Little Miami, 2014.

Bronstein, Herbert. *A Passover Haggadah*. Drawings by Leonard Baskin. Rev. ed. New York: Central Conference of American Rabbis, 1994.

Buber, Martin. *Tales of the Hasidim*. Vol. 2, *The Later Masters*. Translated by Olga Marx. New York: Schocken, 1948.

Burpo, Todd, with Lynn Vincent. *Heaven Is for Real: A Little Boy's Astounding Story of His Trip to Heaven and Back*. Nashville: Nelson, 2010.

Cohen, A. *The Psalms: Hebrew Text & English Translation with an Introduction and Commentary*. London: Soncino, 1950.

Frishman, Elyse D., ed. *Mishkan T'filah*. New York: Central Conference of American Rabbis, 2007.

Goldwurm, Hersh, gen. ed. *Talmud Bavli: Tractate Berachos*. Talmud (Schottenstein edition), vols. 1–2. 71 vols. ArtScroll Series. Brooklyn, NY: Mesorah, 1997.

Goor, Donald, ed. *L'Chol Z'man Va-eit, For Sacred Moments: The CCAR Life-Cycle Guide*. New York: Central Conference of American Rabbis, 2015.

Hertz, Joseph H. *The Authorized Daily Prayer Book Hebrew Text, English Translation with Commentary and Notes*. Rev. ed. New York: Bloch, 1971.

JPS Hebrew-English Tanakh: The Traditional Hebrew Text and the New JPS Translation. 2nd ed. Philadelphia: Jewish Publication Society, 1999.

Kravitz, Leonard, and Kerry M. Olitzky, eds. *Pirke Avot: A Modern Commentary on Jewish Ethics*. New York: UAHC, 1993.

Kushner, Harold S. *When Bad Things Happen to Good People*. 2nd ed. New York: Schocken, 1989.

Kushner, Lawrence. *God Was in This Place & I, I Did not Know: Finding Self, Spirituality, and Ultimate Meaning*. Woodstock, VT: Jewish Lights, 1991.

Lamm, Maurice. *The Jewish Way in Death and Mourning*. New York: David, 1969.

Bibliography

Long, Liza. "I Am Adam Lanza's Mother: It's Time to Talk about Mental Illness." *Blue Review*, December 14, 2012. https://thebluereview.org/i-am-adam-lanzas-mother/.

Mandell, Sherri. *The Blessing of a Broken Heart: The Journey of Healing from Horrific Grief*. London: Toby, 2003.

Neusner, Jacob, trans. *The Mishnah: A New Translation*. New Haven: Yale University Press, 1988.

Pausch, Randy, with Jeffrey Zaslow. *The Last Lecture*. New York: Hyperion, 2008.

Polish, David, ed. *Rabbi's Manual*. Historical and Halachic notes by W. Gunther Plaut. New York: Central Conference of American Rabbis, 1988.

Rando, Therese A. *How to Go on Living When Someone You Love Dies*. New York: Bantam, 1991.

Sonsino, Rifat, and Daniel B Syme. *What Happens after I Die? Jewish Views of Life after Death*. New York: UAHC Press, 1990.

Spitz, Elie Kaplan. *Does the Soul Survive? A Jewish Journey to Belief in Afterlife, Past Lives & Living with Purpose*. Woodstock, VT: Jewish Lights, 2001.

Stern, Chaim, ed. *Gates of Prayer: The New Union Prayerbook (Weekdays, Sabbaths, and Festivals): Services and Prayers for Synagogue and Home*. New York: Central Conference of American Rabbis, 1975.

———. *Gates of Repentance: The New Union Prayerbook for the Days of Awe*. New York: Central Conference of American Rabbis, 1978.

Tananbaum, Samantha. *Life Is Like a Box of Chocolates* (blog). December 2012 post.

Telushkin, Joseph. *Words That Hurt, Words That Heal: How to Choose Words Wisely and Well*. New York: Morrow, 1996.

Weems, Ann. *Searching for Shalom: Resources for Creative Worship*. Louisville: Westminster John Knox, 1991.

Wolpe, David J. *Teaching Your Children about God: A Modern Jewish Approach*. New York: Harper Perennial, 1994.